(Re)

Valuing

Cummings

university press of florida

gainesville

tallahassee

tampa

boca raton

pensacola

orlando

miami

jacksonville

(Re)

Valuing

Cummings

:further

es

sa

ys

on the poet,   Norman Friedman

19

62

—

19

93

Copyright 1996 by the Board
of Regents of the State of Florida
Printed in the United States of
America on acid-free paper
All rights reserved
01 00 99 98 97 96 6 5 4 3 2 1
Library of Congress Cataloging-in-
Publication Data
Friedman, Norman.
(Re)valuing Cummings: further essays on
the poet, 1962–1993 / Norman Friedman.
p. cm.
Includes bibliographical references and
index.
ISBN 0-8130-1443-3 (alk. paper)
1. Cummings, E. E. (Edward Estlin),
1894–1962—Criticism and interpretation.
I. Title.
PS3505.U334Z67   1996
811'.52—dc 20   95-46724
The University Press of Florida is the
scholarly publishing agency for the State
University System of Florida, comprised
of Florida A & M University, Florida
Atlantic University, Florida International
University, Florida State University,
University of Central Florida, University
of Florida, University of North Florida,
University of South Florida, and
University of West Florida.
University Press of Florida
15 Northwest 15th Street
Gainesville, FL 32611

Once
again
for
Zelda
and
always

contents

preface

Although I do not think I have finished with Cummings yet, I do think that I have here a selection of my work—published and unpublished—written since my two previous books appeared, that's meaningful enough to present to the reading public in book form. And in particular, since 1994 was the centennial year of Cummings' birth, it would seem especially appropriate to remember the occasion with a collection such as this. Indeed, I am proud and pleased to be able to join my good friend and colleague Richard S. Kennedy, whose *E. E. Cummings Revisited* also appeared recently.

As I was looking over my entire output on Cummings, published and unpublished, beginning with a Harvard class paper and my honors thesis of 1947 and extending up to and including my contribution to the precentennial read-in at the Jefferson Market Library in New York City in October of 1992—a span of forty-five years!—I decided that the writings which preceded my two books of 1960 and 1964 had naturally been more or less absorbed in and superseded by those latter works. A new book should represent, therefore, my best thoughts and feelings *since* that time.

Thus the two earliest essays included date from 1962 and 1964. Nine of the fourteen appeared between 1972 and 1985. The remaining three were either not previously published or were published in the small-circulation journal of the E. E. Cummings Society, *SPRING* (old style). The whole, then, represents subsequent material, while at the same time not being hitherto readily accessible or visible as the unified body of work that it in fact is. The concluding essay has been written especially for this volume.

The main unifying principle is my attempt to outline more clearly than I believe has been done before just what the powers and limitations of Cummings' art are, and why, and to place that attempt in the enriching context of his life and the life of our times—particularly as they relate, of course, to the problems of writing, interpreting, teaching, and reading poetry. I don't believe that I was ready or equipped for that task until after I had put my two previous books into the public record.

Not that I judge those previous books as obsolete: while it is true that my appropriate purpose at that time, because enough had been questioned by enough reputable critics to be at issue, was to show the interested public that Cummings and his work were worthy of serious critical attention, it is also true that in doing so I believe I produced enough valid and useful analysis and interpretation to be still of interest today. My first book contains a detailed explanation of the art of his poetry—its forms, techniques, and devices; my second attempts a fresh interpretation of all of his works, in prose as well as poetry, in chronological order so as to emphasize the growth of the writer; while the present volume aspires to a more complex evaluation of the entire enterprise in the light of the wisdom of hindsight.

My next decision, as to how to *organize* the present book, was resolved when I began to see that the essays meriting inclusion seemed to fall naturally into three groups: those dealing with the art itself, those dealing with his critics, and those dealing with the man and his life as these relate to the art. It also seemed appropriate to arrange these groups in that order, both for the sake of interest as well as of logic, the sequence being work–reception–writer. There is also some logic in arranging them roughly in the order in which they were originally written, so as to preserve the evolution of my own responses.

The final stage arrived when I realized I had to write a concluding chapter to tie up the threads of all that went before and to explain where my thinking is at the present time.

Although the essays forming the basis of this book were originally published mainly in scholarly and critical journals, they are not necessarily limited to a scholarly and critical audience. The framing and editing I have devised, as well as the original thrust itself of these pieces, are aimed at the more general educated public, and especially at that portion of it which is concerned with modern literature and its place in our history and our lives.

Poetry, as Auden wrote in his elegy on Yeats, may make nothing happen, but it does survive, "A way of happening, a mouth." It survives, that is to say, among those of us who care about it, to help inform us of our whereabouts and assist us in finding a direction and a path. At least that has been my experience, however winding and rocky the road has been.

acknowledgments

I want to thank my colleagues, Richard S. Kennedy and David V. Forrest, for their longtime friendship and support. Gratitude is also due Cathy Zafarana and Chris Arcudi for their help in preparing the manuscript. And thanks also go to the following publications for permission to reprint articles of mine that originally appeared in their pages, although sometimes adapted for the present purpose:

Chapter 1 appeared in *Forum* 3, no. 10 (Spring–Summer 1962): 40–46.

Chapters 2 and 10 appeared in *Journal of Modern Literature* 7, no. 2 (April 1979): 295–322.

Chapters 3 and 13 appeared in *SPRING: The Journal of the E. E. Cummings Society* 4, no. 1 (April 1984): 6–7; 5, no. 3 (October 1985): 3–8.

Chapter 4 appeared in Richard Giles, ed., *Hopkins among the Poets: Studies in Response to Gerard Manley Hopkins.* Hamilton, Ontario: International Hopkins Association Monograph Series No. 3 (1985): 47–52.

Chapter 6 appeared in *Criticism* 6, no. 2 (Spring 1964): 114–33.

Chapter 7 appeared as the introduction in Norman Friedman, ed., *E. E. Cummings: A Collection of Critical Essays.* Reprinted by permission of the publisher, Prentice-Hall/A Division of Simon and Schuster, copyright 1972, 1–12.

Chapter 8 appeared in *Resources for American Literary Study* 13, no. 1 (Spring 1983): 10–25, copyright 1983 by The Pennsylvania State University and reproduced by permission of The Pennsylvania State University Press.

Chapters 9 and 12 appeared in *Linguistics and Literature* (now *Language and Literature*) 9 (1984): 1–56.

Chapter 11 appeared in the *Harvard Library Bulletin* 29, no. 2 (April 1981): 117–34.

Acknowledgment is also made to the following authors and publishers for other material reprinted in this volume:

W. H. Auden, excerpt from "September 1, 1939," from *Collected Poems,* copyright 1940 by W. H. Auden and reprinted with permission of Random House, Inc.

E. E. Cummings materials are reprinted by permission of Liveright Publishing Corporation and the E. E. Cummings Copyright Trust, copyright the E. E. Cummings Copyright Trust.

Lloyd N. Dendinger, *E. E. Cummings: The Critical Reception*, 1981, Burt Franklin, New York. Excerpts reprinted by permission of Lloyd N. Dendinger.

T. S. Eliot, excerpt from "The Love Song of J. Alfred Prufrock," from *Collected Poems 1909–1962*, copyright 1962 by Harcourt, Brace. Excerpt from "Little Gidding" in *Four Quartets*, copyright 1943 by T. S. Eliot and renewed 1971 by Esme Valerie Eliot, reprinted by permission. Excerpt from "The Metaphysical Poets" in *Selected Essays* by T. S. Eliot, copyright 1950. Reprinted by permission of Harcourt, Brace and renewed 1978 by Esme Valerie Eliot.

Irene Fairley, excerpts from "Cummings' Love Lyrics: Some Notes by a Female Linguist," *Journal of Modern Literature* 7, no. 2 (April 1979): 205–18.

Norman Friedman, excerpt from *E. E. Cummings: The Growth of a Writer.* Copyright 1964 by Southern Illinois University Press.

Richard S. Kennedy, excerpts from *Dreams in the Mirror: A Biography of E. E. Cummings.* Reprinted by permission of Liveright Publishing Corporation, copyright 1980 by Richard S. Kennedy.

Rushworth Kidder, excerpts from "Cummings and Cubism: The Influence of the Visual Arts on Cummings' Poetry," *Journal of Modern Literature* 7, no. 2 (April 1979): 255–91. Excerpts from *E. E. Cummings: An Introduction to the Poetry*, copyright 1979 by Columbia University Press and reprinted with permission of the publisher.

Thomas Merton, translator, excerpts from *The Way of Chuang Tzu*, 1979, New Directions Publishing Corporation. Reprinted by permission of the publisher.

J. Hillis Miller, excerpts from *The Disappearance of God*, 1963, Harvard University Press.

Charles Norman, excerpts from *Poets & People*, 1972, Bobbs-Merrill. Reprinted by permission of Charles Norman. Excerpts from *E. E. Cummings: The Magic-Maker*, revised edition 1964 by Duell, Sloan, and Pearce, reprinted by permission of Charles Norman.

Ezra Pound, excerpts from *Hugh Selwyn Mauberley*, copyright 1957; excerpts from *The Cantos*, copyright 1934, 1937, 1940, 1948. Reprinted by permission of New Directions Publishing Corporation.

Theodore Roethke, excerpt from "Elegy for Jane," from *The Collected Poems of Theodore Roethke*, copyright 1950. Reprinted by permission of Doubleday, a division of Bantam Doubleday Dell Publishing Group, Inc.

Wallace Stevens, excerpts from "Sunday Morning," from *The Collected Poems of Wallace Stevens*, copyright 1923 and renewed 1951 by Wallace Stevens. Reprinted by permission of Alfred A. Knopf, Inc., a subsidiary of Random House, Inc.

Hildegarde Lasell Watson, excerpts from *The Edge of the Woods*, copyright 1979 by James S. Watson, Jr. and published 1979 by Stinehour Press. Reprinted by permission of Nancy Dean.

Alfred North Whitehead, excerpt from *Science and the Modern World*, copyright 1925, 1939. Reprinted by permission of the Macmillan Company.

William Butler Yeats, excerpt from "A Dialogue of Self and Soul," from *The Poems of William Butler Yeats: A New Edition*, edited by Richard J. Finneran. Copyright 1933 by Macmillan Publishing Company, renewed 1961 by Bertha Georgie Yeats. Reprinted by permission of Simon and Schuster.

part

one

:the

work

1

E. E. Cummings and the Modernist Tradition

Part 1 of this book deals with those aspects of Cummings' work which engaged my attention after the completion of my two earlier full-length studies. The first chapter, originally published in *Forum* in 1962, is a concerted attempt to reconcile the early view of Cummings as an avant-garde modernist with the later criticism of him as lacking irony and paradox.

I

E. E. Cummings occupies an anomalous position in modern poetry. On the one hand, he is often thought of, usually by those hostile to the modernist tradition, as an avant-gardist, an impossibly obscure poet, a leading figure in what Max Eastman once called "the cult of unintelligibility." On the other hand, he is frequently regarded, usually by those committed to the modernist aesthetic, as a romantic, a perpetual adolescent, and a sentimentalist. Now, for a poet whose stance is that of a nonconformist, one whose policy it is to disregard fads, fashions, and reviewers, such an anomaly might not be particularly bad news. As he himself put it, in the author's dialogue with the reader which forms the introduction (1932) to the Modern Library edition (1934) of *The Enormous Room* (1922):

> Ah—but (now that you mention it) [says his interlocutor] isn't love just a trifle oldfashioned?
>
> I dare say [replies the poet].
>
> And aren't you supposed to be ultramodernistic?
>
> I dare say.

But for those of us whose interest lies in trying to understand the varieties of modernist poetry, it might be of some value to look into the causes of this anomaly and thereby to evaluate more justly Cummings' true place in our literature.

I think, to begin with, that there *are* adequate grounds in Cummings' poetry for such apparently contradictory opinions, because his work does contain both modernist and more romantic elements. He is not modern, for example, in his lack of sophistication and ambivalence, in the simplicity and naturalness of his symbolism, in his directness of affirmative statement, and so on. On the other hand, he shares with poets like Yeats, Pound, Stevens, Eliot, and Auden an opposition to scientific rationalism and the commercialistic vulgarity of modern middle-class life, an insistence upon the value of the irrational and intuitive, an interest in technical and stylistic experimentation, a single-minded devotion to the role of the artist and the function of poetry, and so on. But rather than fixing upon one element or the other as characteristic, and then evaluating his work on such a partial basis, I would prefer to attempt an explanation of what is characteristic in terms of the ways in which these two elements are related—and interrelated—in his poetry.

II

But first, let us consider in more detail the ways in which he diverges from the modernist tradition, and the reasons for this divergence. His subjects, for example, differ in content or in treatment, or both, from those of the moderns. Where he is likely to sing of the joys of spring, they are prone to discuss its sorrows; where he praises the insights of childhood, they analyze its conflicts; where he treats of landscapes and seasons in terms of an affirmative vision, they see them as symbols of humanity's alienation. They both share an interest in the wasteland of modern life, but where he sees it as an object of satire, they treat it as a tragic dilemma. They both are concerned with twentieth-century humankind's loss of sexuality and creativity, but where he simply asserts the value of these things, they are caught in the coils of disgust and guilt. Cummings is one of the few poets of his generation, for example, who writes straightforward but serious love poetry. If he exalts the individual, they wonder how the Individual is to be reconciled with Society. Where they trace adult conflicts back to their parents, he writes poems of unashamed filial piety.

If we are realizing more and more that the poor Victorians were as much the poets of doubt as of faith, we have always known that the moderns have tried to make faith out of doubt—as Robert Penn Warren's Willie Stark tried to make good out of evil—because there isn't anything else to make it out of. But there is little doubt in Cummings; his love hasn't a why or because or although: it exists for no reason, and for that reason it cannot be doubted. It is self-contained, self-sufficient, self-creating, and altogether apart from cause and effect. As he explains in his 1946 introduction to George Herriman's *Krazy Kat*:

> Let's make no mistake about Krazy. A lot of people "love" because, and a lot of people "love" although, and a few individuals love. Love is something illimitable; and a lot of people spend their limited lives trying to prevent anything illimitable from happening to them. Krazy, however, is not a lot of people. Krazy is herself. Krazy is illimitable—she loves. She loves in the only way anyone can love: illimitably. She isn't morbid and she isn't longsuffering; she doesn't "love" someone because he hurts her and she doesn't "love" someone although he hurts her. She doesn't, moreover, "love" someone who hurts her. Quite the contrary: she loves someone who gives her unmitigated joy. How? By always trying his limited worst to make her unlove him, and always failing—not that our heroine is insensitive (for a more sensitive heroine never existed), but that our villain's every effort to limit her love with his unlove ends by a transforming of his limitation into her illimitability. (*A Miscellany Revised*, 324–25)

What are the reasons for these differences? The modernists view their complex techniques as attempts to capture in aesthetic form that which is otherwise inexpressible. Cummings' experiments may also be viewed as means to a similar end—only the end is conceived in a somewhat different way in each case, and hence is approached along a rather different route. The modernist's view of the world—and an obsession with the knowledgeable power-world occupies a large portion of that view—is complicated, and the notion of ultimate truth is complex. For them, reality is a many-sided affair, and it is poetry's job to capture that reality. As Eliot explained long ago in his essay on "The Metaphysical Poets" (1921): "We can only say that it appears likely that poets in our civilization, as it exists at present, must be *difficult*. Our civilization comprehends great variety and complexity, and this variety and complexity, playing upon a refined sensibility, must produce various and complex results. The poet must become more and more comprehensive, more allusive, more indirect, in order to force, to dislocate if necessary, language into his meaning."

And this is a job that no other mode of human apprehension and discourse—least of all, science—is fitted for. The modernists' view of poetry, therefore, is correspondingly subtle. They want, on the one hand, to disengage poetry from the necessity of rational verification as well as from the pressures of personal and practical utility, and on the other hand, to endow it with a truth-value and a usefulness of its own. This is done by developing the notion of "another kind of truth" and reformulating the concept of utility. Truth, for the modernist, is not limited to mere matters of fact, but includes as well the ways in which values arise from and modify in turn these matters. This is the way Alfred North Whitehead puts it: "What is wanted is an appreciation of the infinite variety of vivid values achieved by an organism in its proper environment. When you understand all about the sun and all about the atmosphere and all about the rotation of the earth, you may still miss the radiance of the sunset. There is no substitute for the direct perception of the concrete achievement of a thing in its actuality. We want concrete fact with a high light thrown on what is relevant to its preciousness" (*Science and the Modern World,* chapter 13).

Reality, then, is in this view no single thing, and no single approach will therefore ever grasp the whole of it. As Yeats wrote at the end of his life: "It seems to me that I have found what I wanted. When I try to put all into a phrase I say, 'Man can embody truth but he cannot know it.'" If it is the job of the poem to embody insights into this reality, then it cannot be confined to any single attitude. And a whole host of devices have been developed to capture this complexity. There is, to begin with, the modernist's obsession with the expressive powers of language and the ways in which these powers may be increased. Connotation, suggestion, irony, ambiguity—these are some of the terms used to examine and discuss such powers. There is, secondly, a similar concern with diction and rhythm, with tone and texture. There is, thirdly, an interest in figures of speech and symbols as ways of multiplying meanings and tapping more primitive levels of awareness. There is, fourthly, the suppression of connectives and transitions in order to preserve uncontaminated the essential poetry of a poem and to avoid the rational and the logical.

And there is, finally and most characteristically, the development of a new concept of the poetic speaker known as the "mask," in which every protagonist is conceived of as containing the opposite, even as having a built-in self-mocker. In this way is the poem disengaged from the private personality of the poet and objectified. The speaker in Yeats' "Sailing to Byzantium," for example, while turning his mind to immortal things, can at the same time see himself from the opposite perspective as "but a paltry thing, / A tattered coat upon a stick." Or Pound's Mauberley, while dedicating himself to art, can simultaneously say of himself:

> "I was
> And I no more exist;
> Here drifted
> An hedonist."

Or Eliot's Prufrock can lament, even as he toys with the idea of doing something heroic:

> And I have seen the eternal Footman hold my coat, and snicker,
> And in short, I was afraid.

Or Auden's speaker, as he concludes a noble reflection about love as the cure for the evils coming to a head in "September 1, 1939," can say:

> May I, composed like them
> Of Eros and of dust,
> Beleagured by the same
> Negation and despair,
> Show an affirming flame.

Or Roethke's speaker can say, as he mourns the death of a student he loved:

> Over this damp grave I speak the words of my love:
> I, with no rights in this matter,
> Neither father nor lover.
>   ("Elegy for Jane")

In each case there is this characteristic double view, this undercutting, this deliberate acknowledgment of one's more foolish side, this insistence upon the un- or anti-heroic.

Complex reality: complex poem. Tension, conflict, reconciliation of opposites, ambivalence, metaphor, drama, paradox—these are basic terms of modernist criticism. The poem is an image of reality and a heuristic device—for it has utility in that it teaches us how to see—as well as an organic and "useless" aesthetic object, reflexive, severed from the poet, self-generating, and indivisible. Thus has the modernist attempted to resolve the ancient form/content dilemma: What is said in the poem is not what it "means," for what it means is inseparable from the *way* it is said. John Ciardi's 1960 poetry textbook is called, with calculated intent, *How Does a Poem Mean?*—not, you may notice, *what* does a poem mean? When all is indirect, readers have to infer the meaning for themselves, and since they must make such inferences on the basis of the total context, then it may be said that the meaning is inseparable from that context. Thus a prose paraphrase can never equal the poem, for it is precisely the way in which a poem's meanings are *embodied* that gets left behind in the abstraction which is paraphrase. So it is said that poetry is what is lost in translation.

But Cummings' picture of the world is somewhat different, and so his techniques vary accordingly in their nature and function. Or perhaps I ought to say "worlds," for in the introduction to *The Enormous Room* he remarks: "I live in so many: which one do you mean?" His interlocutor replies: "I mean the everyday humdrum world, which includes me and you and millions upon millions of men and women." This is a distinction resembling that between the sensical and knowledgeable power-world of Offissa Pup and Ignatz Mouse, and the nonsensical world of love inhabited by Krazy Kat. The point in Cummings is that to lose the two-dimensional everyday world is to gain the three-dimensional world of understanding. This is a world without conflict, where hope has no opposite in fear; a world without contingency, without compromise, without contradiction, without limits, and without fixity. It is the world of what's possible and hence is the source of all our values. It is the world which Cummings refers to as "dream," "magic," "mystery," and "miracle."

It is the world, in short, which gives meaning and significance to our everyday humdrum world. Evil—and he sees plenty of it around him, for he is no naive optimist—exists in this latter world, but for him it is the result of a corrupt will rather than an inherent part of the universe. Fear is what corrupts that will, and love is what cures it—this it does by a paradoxical surrender, for a loss of self is a loss of fear. It's not so much, therefore, that he sees reality as simplistic, as that he doesn't see the good and the bad as necessarily intertwined. His world is complicated, but his vision of it is not complex.

And his view of poetry is correspondingly dichotomous. The persuasion by the lover who urges his lady to accept the three-dimensional freedom of surrender, and the castigation by the critic who deplores a two-dimensional man's voluntary slavery to his fears—these are the poles of his poetry, the lyric and the satire:

> you shall above all things be glad and young.
> For if you're young,whatever life you wear
>
> it will become you;and if you are glad
> whatever's living will yourself become. . . .
>> (*New Poems*, #22)

> when god decided to invent
> everything he took one
> breath bigger than a circustent
> and everything began
>
> when man determined to destroy
> himself he picked the was
> of shall and finding only why
> smashed it into because
>> (*1 x 1*, #XXVI)

These, plus descriptions of and reflections on landscapes and seasons, which open, as we shall see, gateways to the infinite. For Cummings, as much as the modernist, conceives also of "another kind of truth."

Nor is his conception of poetic form any less "organic." For it is no necessary part of a theory which holds that form and content are inseparable to require ambivalence, irony, and the rest. A poem may aim at a single affirmative expression and still depend upon the way it does so for its proper significance to be grasped. That which is inexpressible may be inexpressible not so much because it is complex as because it is ineffable. If Cummings has shown no interest in the modernist lyric mask, in the techniques of discontinuity, in mythic symbols, he has explored—even more deeply than the modernists—certain possibilities of language. These are, specifically, the grammatical shift, syntactic disarrangement, experiments in the free-verse stanza, and the mingling of different levels of diction. To these devices he has added certain others of his own: the controversial typographic displacements, and the unconventional handling of punctuation and capitalization.

Aside from causing what is said to be inseparable from the way it is said, these devices, rather than serving as subtle nets to snare the elusive variety and complexity of the everyday world, function instead to make the reader see and feel and understand directly and immediately the nonsensical world of love. To change the word order radically, for example, or to break words typographically, prevents the reader from following a sentence rationally and consecutively, so that when he does see the pattern, he grasps it all at once rather than abstractly from point to point. "I am abnormally fond of that precision which creates movement," Cummings says in the foreword to *is* 5. Such techniques do not communicate meanings; they provoke insights. As the introduction to *Krazy Kat* puts it: "We understand that, just as there is something—love—infinitely more significant than brute force, there is something—wisdom—infinitely more significant than mental prowess. A remarkably developed intelligence impresses us about as much as a sixteen-inch bicep. If we know anything, we know that a lot of people can learn knowledge (which is the same thing as unlearning ignorance) but that no one can learn wisdom. Wisdom, like love, is a spiritual gift" (*A Miscellany Revised*, 325).

In one sense, then, Cummings' problem is the reverse of the modernists': rather than framing a complex mirror to reflect a complex reality, he is treating simple subjects and attitudes in a complicated way. And the complication is an attempt to freshen what might otherwise be taken as an ordinary idea and to wake it up for us. There are many themes that we have taken so much for granted that they have become clichés, and it is these clichés which the modernist avoids like the plague. The work of Cummings represents an alternative course, for he has undertaken to drain the swamps themselves: a cliché is not necessarily false because people no longer think or feel while uttering it. To love one's mate wholeheartedly, to revere one's parents, to look back with gratification upon one's childhood, to say joyous things at the arrival of spring, to praise the individual—to do these things places one in imminent danger indeed of falling into the heart of clichéland itself. But to say that Cummings' well-known poem on his father reminds one, as a certain reviewer has done, of a *Reader's Digest* "Most Unforgettable Character I've Ever Met" sketch is simply to ignore the way the poem is written in favor of its message:

> though dull were all we taste as bright,
> bitter all utterly things sweet,
> maggoty minus and dumb death
> all we inherit,all bequeath
>
> and nothing quite so least as truth
> —i say though hate were why men breathe—
> because my father lived his soul
> love is the whole and more than all
> (*50 Poems*, #34)

But isn't it a central modernist doctrine that poetic excellence derives not intrinsically from the poem's subject but rather from its *treatment* of the subject? In this way modernism supports and confirms its notion of organic form, for if certain subjects are more "poetical" than others, then form and content *are* separable. Thus has modernism argued for the extension of poetic subject matters to include the nonpoetic and the anti-poetic, the ugly, the sordid, and the shocking. Thus has it managed its separation of poetry from the comparatively crude pressures of conventional morality. For it believes in the power of the artistic imagination to transform and give significance to any subject, however unpromising or unconventional. And modernism is right. Why, therefore, should it deny this power to the poet's vision when it comes to the cliché?

For Cummings' problem is to say what has been said to death. Those, however, who confuse his love lyrics with the verses on Valentine cards are committing the "heresy of paraphrase," they are victims of the stock response:

> never could anyone
> who simply lives to die
> dream that your valentine
> makes happier me than i
>
> but always everything
> which only dies to grow
> can guess and as for spring
> she'll be the first to know
> (*95 Poems*, #46)

He is saying things which sound familiar but are no longer familiar when he gets through with them. It is the difference between hypocrisy and the

real thing, the meretricious and the genuine, the commercial and the creative: on the surface both might look alike and a description of each might
even sound alike, but each is held together on entirely different principles.
When Cummings talks about love he may sound to the inattentive reader
like Cole Porter, but he is not only actually feeling what he is talking about,
he is also talking about it in an entirely fresh way:

> i carry your heart with me(i carry it in
> my heart)i am never without it(anywhere
> i go you go,my dear;and whatever is done
> by only me is your doing,my darling). . . .
>   (95 *Poems*, #92)

What redeems this poem from ordinariness is the distinction of its language—to be found in its delicacy and balance of phrasing, in its purity of
tone, and in its careful management of the sonnet form—and the depth of
its source in a profoundly mystical view of life, implied in the concept of
"fate" and "world" as well as in the tree–root–bud imagery toward the end.

So, when you come right down to it, what we thought was only too familiar turns out to be actually ineffable. The manner of expression *is* inseparable from what is being expressed: if he talks in a way no one ever
thought of before, then what he is saying represents what is difficult to feel
under ordinary conditions also. His poetry is not merely what oft was thought
but ne'er so well expressed, after all. Draining the swamps of cliché-land
takes us into the heart of the mystery. For what *is* love anyway? Or innocence, for that matter? Or an individual? Are we really weary of these themes
because they are so boringly obvious? Or because we have trouble grasping
them, and always have?

III

Thus, in another sense, the complexity of Cummings' techniques represents an attempt to express the inexpressible. And here he joins the modernists in a common enterprise. For the ultimate aim of poets like Yeats,
Pound, Stevens, Eliot, and Auden is to achieve a "unification of sensibility," a vision of the timeless moment. The net result of attempting to express the variety and complexity of a various and complex world, of aiming
at a sense of the concrete thing in its vivid and varied actuality, is unity—
the unity of a vision which transcends, without excluding, variety. This is

truly another kind of truth, a kind which science not only does not, but also cannot, duplicate. For science, although it may aspire to a unified field theory, can only do so in terms of its own proper limits: in being necessarily bound to the measurable and the verifiable, it can never approach the immeasurable and the intuitive. And the transcendent vision of the poet is of the immeasurable and the intuitive. The modernist movement, often castigated as being negative and dehumanizing, may be properly understood only in terms of its culminating affirmation. Here, for example, is the conclusion of Yeats' "A Dialogue of Self and Soul":

> When such as I cast out remorse
> So great a sweetness flows into the breast
> We must laugh and we must sing,
> We are blest by everything,
> Everything we look upon is blest.

Or the conclusion of Eliot's *Four Quartets*:

> Quick now, here, now, always—
> A condition of complete simplicity
> (Costing not less than everything)
> And all shall be well and
> All manner of thing shall be well
> When the tongues of flame are in-folded
> Into the crowned knot of fire
> And the fire and the rose are one.

Or the still point at the center of Pound's *Cantos,* in Canto XLIX:

> Sun up; work
> sundown; to rest
> dig well and drink of the water
> dig field; eat of the grain
> Imperial power is? and to us what is it?

> The fourth; the dimension of stillness.
> And the power over wild beasts.

Or the lovely conclusion of Stevens' "Sunday Morning":

> Deer walk upon our mountains, and the quail
> Whistle about us their spontaneous cries;

> Sweet berries ripen in the wilderness;
> And, in the isolation of the sky,
> At evening, casual flocks of pigeons make
> Ambiguous undulations as they sink,
> Downward to darkness, on extended wings.

Both the modernist and Cummings are, in the end, striving for the transcendental vision. For Cummings, too, it is the result of a direct perception of the concrete thing. Here is #48 of 95 *Poems*:

> someone i am wandering a town(if its
> houses turning into themselves grow
> silent upon new perfectly blue)
>
> i am any(while around him streets
> taking moment off by moment day
> thankfully become each other(one who
> feels a world crylaughingly float away
>
> leaving just this strolling ghostly doll
> of an almost vanished me(for whom
> the departure of everything real is the
> arrival of everything true)and i'm
>
> no(if deeply less conceivable than
> birth or death or even than breathing shall
>
> blossom a first star)one

The basic, the real difference between them is that, while modernists feel they must reach this vision only after long struggle and much difficulty, Cummings may go right to it directly. For the modernists, direct perception refers to the two-dimensional world we live in every day, while for Cummings it refers to the immortal natural world in terms of which we may grasp the three-dimensional world of understanding. For them a transcendent insight is the result of deliberate discipline; for him it is a felt experience. The modernists achieve it by a painful dialectic process of balancing tensions, and for them it is difficult to surrender; Cummings achieves it by immediate intuition, and for him to surrender is joyful. What they are seeking, he already has.

This means that the modernists want to achieve unity without giving up anything—without surrendering, for example, their maturity of outlook with its sad knowledge of how good and evil are rarely a matter of black and white. As we have seen, they hedge their bets. They want a vision of infinite possibility without surrendering their tragic sense of the inevitability of failure and of their self-involvement in the will of fate. They want the Just City on earth to pave the way to the Heavenly City above; they want to remain in History while living outside of Time. They want to rediscover and awaken the primitive levels of being without discarding Civilization and Culture. They want to achieve the three-dimensional world without surrendering the two-dimensional world.

Now this indeed results in a "dramatic" sort of poetry, in an especially *human* sort of poetry, and I would be the last to wish it away. It is, in effect, the poetry of the modern intellectual, having had a wide appeal among modern intellectuals, but its difficulty kept it from having wider appeal. Certainly Eliot, for one, yearned all along for a larger audience, and he took in his later years to decrying (the final irony!) the isolation of modern poetry among academic coteries and recommending that it be removed from the curriculum and be read simply for fun. Modern poetry is certainly, from my experience, popular among undergraduates. It speaks frankly to us about what we must be feeling, and even teaches us what we ought to be feeling. It proposes to face the difficult world we live in without flinching, and the solution to our problems it offers is not an easy one—to be achieved, if at all, only after much effort. It is, in short, about *us*. For we find it hard to give up the knowledgeable power-world, too.

Indeed, the modernist objection to Cummings is based upon the modernist assumption that the affirmative vision has to be "earned." Cummings, it is said, is naive and sentimental because his affirmation came early and stayed late. His career does not seem to be marked by that climax of spiritual conversion found in the careers of poets like Yeats, Eliot, and Auden (although no such pattern is found in the careers of Frost, Stevens, and Pound, for example). He does not seem to struggle through the darkness toward the light, apparently being born knowing what he knows. And thus he is called a perpetual adolescent. (That the case is somewhat more involved will emerge in subsequent chapters.)

Cummings does not hedge his bets. He is not obsessed with the "mature sensibility," because he knows that is just what sells us out in a pinch. He is not weighed down by the tragic vision because he knows we create our fate. Failure doesn't stymie him because he has accepted it from the start as a condition of freedom. He is not concerned with History and the City because he knows that when people act in groups they are motivated by abstractions. He is not in pursuit of the primitive because he *is* a primitive, and he knows that if Culture doesn't come naturally, it had better not come at all.

His is not a poetry about us and our situation. Isn't there something more difficult after all in such a poetry, a poetry which comes telling us we can be different? And hasn't the divided self been in manifest danger of becoming in turn a stock response, the modern cliché?

IV

So if the two common opinions are both right in saying that Cummings is a romanticist and a modernist, we have seen that these elements are not so simply defined as we had thought. Neither really understands him, but each misunderstands him differently. It is in the way modernism and romanticism are intertwined that the essence of his work is to be found. His "romantic" vision turns out to be ultimately modern, while his "modern" techniques turn out after all not to be the ones favored by the modernists. Having to express what is equally inexpressible, he is equally experimental. But his techniques vary from theirs in that, while his vision has the same goal as theirs, his tends to begin where theirs leaves off.

Neither the modernist nor Cummings, however, has sold us short about one thing: neither has committed the old Victorian error of needing to see the transcendent in terms of absolutes, in terms of abstractions. No systems, no dogmas of the supernatural have been erected to take the place of our vanished certitudes. Both have realized that what killed religion was not its dogmas but rather the fact that it *took* them as dogmas. Although both deplore what middle-class vulgarity has made of the world, neither tells us the old lie that the natural world is unreal. As the modernist tells us that no formulation of the transcendent is or can be final—

> Shall she not find in comforts of the sun,
> In pungent fruit and bright, green wings, or else
> In any balm or beauty of the earth,
> Things to be cherished like the thought of heaven?
>   (Stevens, "Sunday Morning")

—so Cummings shows us that the never-changing infinite can only be found in the ever-changing finite:

> luminous tendril of celestial wish
> (whying diminutive bright deathlessness
> to these my not themselves believing eyes
> adventuring,enormous nowhere from)
>
> querying affirmation;virginal
>
> immediacy of precision:more
> and perfectly more most ethereal
> silence through twilight's mystery made flesh—
>
> dreamslender exquisite white firstful flame
>
> —new moon!as(by the miracle of your
> sweet innocence refuted)clumsy some
> dull cowardice called a world vanishes,
>
> teach disappearing also me the keen
> illimitable secret of begin
>   (*Xaipe*, #71)

If modernism does not often delight in the physical world as Cummings does, being torn by its transiency and its mortality, it nevertheless will not forsake it, and in the end blesses it too. As modernism constantly shifts its ground, so Cummings says:

> never to rest and never to have:only to grow.
> Always the beautiful answer who asks a more beautiful question
>   (Introduction to *Collected Poems*, 1938)

If life can be said to have a secret, and if that secret can be expressed in words, then this is it. Even a faith such as Cummings' is never fixed, never final. Each poem for him is a new beginning, but neither evil nor old age nor death are ever far from his sight as he sings afresh of the familiar but inscrutable glory of love:

> being to timelessness as it's to time,
> love did no more begin than love will end;
> where nothing is to breathe to stroll to swim
> love is the air the ocean and the land

(do lovers suffer?all divinities
proudly descending put on deathful flesh:
are lovers glad?only their smallest joy's
a universe emerging from a wish)

love is the voice under all silences,
the hope which has no opposite in fear;
the strength so strong mere force is feebleness:
the truth more first than sun more last than star

—do lovers love?why then to heaven with hell.
Whatever sages say and fools,all's well
                    (95 *Poems*, #94)

2

Cummings Posthumous I

:The Works

Richard Kennedy took on the task in the late 1970s of editing a Cummings issue of the *Journal of Modern Literature*, and he kindly asked me to contribute a piece. My thought was to continue and complete my book-by-book account of Cummings' literary career past the point reached in my 1964 volume—which, as it happens, was being written just before the poet's untimely death in 1962. The publications to be considered, then—with the exception of *Selected Letters* as being more suitable for the third part of this book—were those which appeared after that time.

I

Apart from *Complete Poems 1913–1962*, which was not published until 1972 but contains nothing except 73 *Poems* not already in book form within the dates of the title, three Cummings volumes were published after his death in 1962: *Adventures in Value* (1962), 73 *Poems* (1963), and *Fairy Tales* (1965). Do these add significantly to his *oeuvre*? Do they tell us anything about him that we didn't know before?

Before addressing myself to these questions, I want to explain in what order I treat these works, for the order of their posthumous publication does not necessarily reflect the order of their composition.

Fairy Tales contains four tales, three of which were published originally in *Wake* between 1946 and 1950.[1] But they appear to have been written much earlier, as Marion Morehouse Cummings explains on the dedicatory page: "These tales were written for Cummings' daughter, Nancy, when she was a very little girl." Now, since Nancy—the child of Cummings' first marriage, which was to Elaine Orr—was born in 1919, the tales would have been written sometime before the mid-twenties.

Adventures in Value, containing fifty photographs by Marion Morehouse, with captions by Cummings, was, to the best of my knowledge, the last published work of Cummings for which he saw the proofs.

73 Poems contains at least forty-six poems which first appeared in magazines while Cummings was still alive, and it does represent as a whole poems which he regarded as completed. The copyrights go back as far as 1950 but mainly fall between 1958 and 1963. Since the preceding book of verse, *95 Poems*, was published in 1958, *73 Poems* seems to represent work done primarily in his last four years. An analysis of this book, then, will provide a fitting climax for this chapter.

II

Like many of his other writings in prose, Cummings' *Fairy Tales* are remarkable for their careful balance—in style and in plot structure. What is equally remarkable is that, in being written openly for children, they are entirely free of coyness and cuteness. And yet they are brilliantly successful, it seems to me, as stories for the young. That is because Cummings takes them absolutely seriously, in that they derive from the same vision which informs his work for adults: an open and receptive attitude toward existence, a lovingness toward individuals, and an emphasis upon spiritual self-dependency. Naturally, we could just as easily turn this argument around and say that his adult vision is remarkable for its emphasis on the child's view of things, but either way we gain, for he takes that with absolute seriousness as well.

"The Old Man Who Said 'Why'" is the most explicitly close to Cummings' other writings. In it, a faerie guru who lives on the farthest star is challenged to investigate a strange old man who has settled on the moon and who is driving all the other denizens of the air crazy by saying "why" all the time. So the guru must go and confront this man "with little green eyes and a big white beard and delicate hands like a doll's hands." But every time the guru asks him a question, the man says, simply, "Why?"—until finally, exasperated beyond endurance, the faerie threatens him, saying, "if you say why again,you'll fall from the moon all the way to the earth." And sure enough, of course, "the little very old man smiled;and looking at the faerie,he said 'why?' and he fell millions and millions and millions of deep cool new beautiful miles(with every part of a mile he became a little younger;first he became a not very old man and next a middle-aged man and then a young man and a boy and finally a child)until,just as he gently touched the earth,he was about to be born."

I am reminded of Wordsworth's immortality ode and of Cummings' "when god decided to invent."

The questioner of this tale is, in the words of the introduction to the 1938 *Collected Poems*, certainly one for whom "birth is a supremely welcome mystery,the mystery of growing," and the image of his turning from an old man into a younger man and then into an infant is exquisite. Recall these lines from "anyone lived in a pretty how town":

> children guessed(but only a few)
> and down they forgot as up they grew
> (50 *Poems*, #29)

"The Elephant and the Butterfly" and "The House That Ate Mosquito Pie" are both about the pure love of a larger, clumsier creature for a smaller, winged creature, which is happily reciprocated. Probably written a quarter-century later than the others, the first is an almost unmarred idyll, with no threat or obstacle standing in the way except the elephant's lack of adventurousness. But the butterfly (who is, interestingly, also a "he")[2] comes to visit him, and they become friends. Then "the elephant put his arm very gently around the little butterfly and said: 'Do you love me a little?' / And the butterfly smiled and said: 'No, I love you very much.'" So the elephant visits the butterfly's house, and the latter asks, "Why didn't you ever before come down into the valley where I live?" And the elephant answered, "Because I did nothing all day." But now he comes to visit every day, "And they loved each other always."

The other story concerns an empty house who is visited by a bird and who invites her to stay and live with him. They plan to make mosquito pie for lunch but are interrupted by the arrival of three people who come by and want to move into the house. This threat is only momentary, however, as the house causes all his clocks to strike at once and scare the people away. Then he and his newfound love can enjoy their lunch and their lives alone.

Cummings' daughter was taken from him sometime after his first marriage broke up, as we shall have occasion to discuss later in this book, but they were later reacquainted. Charles Norman reports, in his memoirs,[3] that Cummings told him the following story just after World War II: "A year or two before, while at his New Hampshire farm, he passed on the road near his house a young woman he did not know and who did not know him. In the country manner both said 'Good morning.' This occurred several mornings on his walks; he saw that she was a visitor at the farm next to his, which belonged to the family of William James. The young woman was his daughter by his first wife. She had been brought up under another name. She had since learned who her father was, and there had been a reunion at Patchin Place." Norman sees this experience, which seems to have the elements of a Greek tragedy, as being reflected in Cummings' *Santa Claus* (1946), where the girl recognizes Santa Claus even though he has exchanged masks with Death, but without knowing he is also her father.

This seems plausible, and I also think it is quite possible that, when Cummings was writing these fairy tales, he was either losing or had just lost his daughter, and that they therefore reflect his fantasy of being able to be with her and win her back.[4] Certainly these tales are effective enough to stand on their own, but they gain added dimension, poignancy, and significance in the biographical context. And there *is* the recurrent motif of the larger and smaller creatures falling in love to be accounted for.

"The Little Girl Named I" carries on this motif in a much more complex and interesting fashion. Here the larger creature is a narrator, and he is telling a story about a little girl to a real little girl. The little girl of the story is named "I," and the form of the frame is that of a dialogue between the narrator and his listener as he tells his tale. The structure of the story itself consists of a series of encounters between "I" and various creatures, as she looks unsuccessfully for a companion to have for tea. She meets a yellow cow, a white horse, a pink pig, and an elephant, but they are all busy doing something else. She continues on alone after each encounter, until finally she "sees another little girl just like her," who turns out to be just the companion she is seeking.

What the frame accomplishes is to show how the teller and the listener gradually shift roles. During the first two encounters, he asks her what she encounter she gets it wrong. Then, during the fourth and fifth encounters, *she* asks the questions and he does the answering. What happens at the end is that they all—the teller, his listener, and the two little girls in the story proper—become one. "And then I said to this other little girl, just like this I said 'Who are you?' / And what did this other little girl say? / 'You. That's who I am' she said 'And You is my name because I'm You.' . . . So then You and I, we went to my house together to have some tea" (39). Recall "Him" and "Me" of Cummings' early play; recall "little you-i" of his poem "o by the by" (1 x 1, #LIII); recall "For love are in you am in i are in we" of "the great advantage of being alive" (*Xaipe*, #66). Doesn't this tale join father and daughter in love through a luncheon, as the house and his bird were joined through their shared mosquito pie, and doesn't it say that you and I, we have only ourselves to count on?

III

Adventures in Value is divided into four sections: EFFIGIES, which contains six photographs; STILL LIFE, which contains eight; NATURE, containing twenty-five; and PEOPLE, with eleven. Three epigraphs stand at the head of the volume: dictionary definitions of "value"; the Emerson quote about society being in conspiracy against the manhood of its members; and the puzzling attribution of a modern-sounding quote to Homer: "I have never tried to do anything but get the proper relationship of values." Marion Morehouse's pictures are for the most part clear, textured close-ups, in sharp focus and stark black and white. Her images are hard, shiny, and thick, and characteristically of burlap, wood, porcelain, rock, frond, vegetable, and light and shadow. Curiously, for a collaboration with a poet who celebrates growth, process, and movement, her photographs are generally without motion—and this is as true of NATURE and PEOPLE as it is of EFFIGIES and STILL LIFE.

Cummings' captions are sometimes about the photograph, sometimes reflections triggered by the picture, and sometimes both. When he directs attention to the picture itself, as in II 4, "Composition," a still life of cooking utensils in front of a wooden wall, he will say, "note the nail." When he takes off from the photograph, he explains, comments, interprets, and reminisces. These, of course, will be our primary concern as readers of Cummings. For other pictures he supplies appropriate quotations, and some he simply leaves blank.

For I 4, "The Mountain (Lachaise)," for example, which shows a small statue of a reclining nude, partially obscured by shadow and branches of blossoms issuing from a vase in the back, Cummings writes, "blossoms & sculpture(impermanence incarnate & intrinsic immortality)now fortunately coexist:now the miracle of the alive touches the mystery of the timeless — nothing can add to or subtract from so true a marriage of the multitudinous & the singular;so beautiful a collision of the momentary and the deathless." Seeing the content of the picture and its relationships in almost schematically symbolic terms, he adds movement to a static configuration — "coexist," "touches," "marriage," and even "collision" — and produces thereby a high moment of integration and transcendence of the polarities.

Number I 6, "Monster," shows a maimed statue of a strange animal inside the fence of the Cluny Museum in Paris. Cummings reflects that three mothers, each with a child, were standing behind this statue not long before. Then he recalls an earlier mother and child: "Paris isn't any longer Paris to someone who remembers sitting on the terrace of a diminutive restaurant . . . & gazing with reverential joy at a lady between ladies:very much the loveliest mother,& by far the livingest child." I cannot help but think that this is yet another reference to his first wife and their daughter, and as I look at the "cheerful maimedness" of this statue, I seem to see the baffled spirit of the father in Cummings looking out at us.

"Sunlight As Joy" is the title of III 1, and we are now in the NATURE section. Here we see a translucent shot of forest leaves in the sun, and Cummings' caption is an epigrammatic statement of his transcendent vision: "joy being a mystery at right angles equally to pain & pleasure,as truth is to fact & fiction." I am reminded of the poem, "hate blows a bubble of despair into," whose second stanza is as follows:

> pleasure and pain are merely surfaces
> (one itself showing,itself hiding one)
> life's only and true value neither is
> love makes the little thickness of the coin
> (50 *Poems*, #43)

"ΕΛΕΦΑΣ" is the title of III 4, and it is a picture of a large rock in front of a pair of birch trees. In his celebration of this presence, Cummings quotes Isak Dinesen: "a being mighty and powerful beyond anyone's attack, attacking no one." Which foreshadows the Tao-like verses accompanying the photograph of Marianne Moore: "in a cruel world — to show mercy / in a hateful world—to forgive" (IV 3). And in III 16 he sees Don Quixote in a pod of milkweed, remarking that here "he's his own Sancho."

But the serenity of these lucidities is crossed, as it is in the letters (and in the published writings), by Cummings' equally characteristic crankiness. In III 8 he manages to move from a picture of a quiet zucchini to yet another attack on the noisy radio. In III 15 he breathes a sigh of relief, over a picture of Patchin Place, that his New York residence has not yet been supplanted by a high-rise, and he proceeds to lambast the otherwise topsy-turvy world. And in "MOIPA" (III 23), he contrasts the eyes that think with those that feel, and says the former have hands that can cut across a tree trunk with a buzz saw.

Then, in the PEOPLE section, he writes a series of captions which celebrate—of all things—hard work. Recalling his earlier poem, "old mr ly" (1 x 1, #XXVII), in connection with a photograph of Old Mr. Lyman (IV 6), he says, "During fifty years he worked—when loafing wasn't mankind's sole aim—hard & well,on behalf of a railroad." "Minnie (1)" (IV 7) is a portrait of a country woman—"no harder working woman ever lived"—who voted, as Cummings assured her he would too, against Franklin D. Roosevelt. Cummings also admires John Finley (IV 9), the Harvard classicist, who "cheerfully toils in the sweat of his brow under skies which freeze or burn" when working on his New England farm. "Jess" (IV 11), then 75, worked harder than the young fellows, "Because work has disappeared from their world." This is in the tradition of "rain or hail," the poem which follows "old mr ly" in 1 x 1, but without the derogation of the rest of the world:

> sam was a man
> grinned his grin
> done his chores
> laid him down.

And so the iconoclastic poet, who celebrated the boulevards, bistros, bordellos, circuses, and burlesque shows of Boston, New York, and Paris as a cosmopolitan young man, and who once proclaimed in a poem that "must's a schoolroom in the month of may" (1 x 1, #XXXIV), retreats finally into a celebration of the Horatian—not to say Calvinistic—rustic, homely virtues and looks with dismay at the moral deterioration of the world he is leaving behind. His rebellion against the hairless old, thwarted when young, now turns itself against the new.[5] And I think these captions give some further clues to the meaning of the Republicanism he espoused in his later years.

His politics had become a form of agrarian, New England Republicanism, where the industrious and isolated farmer feels in his bones that the government which governs least is indeed the best. He believes in the "character"-laden efforts of the worthy individual, and he will have no truck with government attempts to better the lot of the unworthy—that is, those who don't work hard. Clearly, these anarchistic planks have only a remote connection with the platform of national Republicanism, with its support of large corporations and a strong military establishment. But since presidential elections are perforce national elections, the confusion of values involved here is noteworthy.

IV

Although 73 *Poems* is made up of work that Cummings himself considered completed before his death, the *order* of poems in this volume is subject to some question. Charles Norman writes in his memoirs[6] that the poet's widow asked him "to edit the poems Cummings had been putting together before he died." This was in 1963: "I worked on the manuscript from April 19 to April 24. It was arranged in a manner Cummings himself might have followed: three sections comprising 'Portraits,' 'Impressions,' and 'Sonnets.' Mrs. Cummings sent the manuscript to Harcourt, Brace & World." But then something went wrong. Norman was also working on the second edition of his biography of the poet and offered as a courtesy to let her see the new last chapter. After reading it, "She was furious. She objected violently to it. She objected most of all to the confidential remark Cummings had made to me in 1961 while waiting for the car that was to take them to the airport." He explained that "it was the kind of remark a man would make to his friend, but not to his wife, who might understandably be upset."

The remark in question, as recorded in *E. E. Cummings: The Magic-Maker*,[7] is "All I ask is one more year." Norman's memoirs continue, "She said that Cummings had not made the remark attributed to him in my chapter, and that I was a liar." She asked Norman to delete it, but he refused. "A few days later I received from her, in addition to my manuscript, a note . . . :Harcourt, Brace & World had found it 'too difficult' to set up Last Poems [Norman's original suggestion for the title] in my arrangement, and the book had been given another format, with the original title [Mrs. Cummings'] restored."

I do not know whether Cummings himself might have followed Norman's suggested order (although his poems *are* roughly classifiable along something like those lines, he had not used such divisions for organizing his books since his three earliest volumes, all of which derive from the original *Tulips and Chimneys* manuscript), but there is a useful clue in his *Selected Letters*. Here Cummings says, in writing to Francis Steegmuller in 1959: "all my booksofpoems after the original T&C manuscript . . . start with autumn(downgoing,despair)& pass through winter(mystery,dream)&stop in spring(upcoming,joy). But as I glance over the index of Poems '23-'54,find few hints of this progression;beyond a tendency to begin dirty(world: sordid,satires)& end clean(earth:lyrical,love-poems)." He sees this as a seasonal metaphor, which he says 95 *Poems* exemplifies clearly, and interprets it via S. Foster Damon's study of Blake: "'They' the angels 'descend on the material side . . . and ascend on the spiritual;this is . . . a representation of the greatest Christian mystery,a statement of the secret every mystic tries to tell'" (261).

The story told in a letter to me by George J. Firmage, Cummings' editor, complements and clarifies that related by Norman. It seems that Mrs. Cummings had asked Firmage to take charge of the manuscript in early December of 1962—which was *before*, of course, Norman received it. At that time, Firmage was not concerned about its ultimate sequential arrangement. He returned the results of his work to Mrs. Cummings in February of 1963 and did not hear from her again until the last week in April. Apparently she had given the manuscript to Norman and subsequently asked for it back during the interim. Firmage got the manuscript once again during the first week in May, and he "made no attempt to imitate Estlin's previously published booksofpoems in arranging the 73 poems that I had to work with; but merely tried, as best I could, to find a pleasing reading order. There was, if I remember correctly, some attempt to move from sunrise to sunset, from light to dark; but the movement is not, as I see it now, consistent." Mrs. Cummings then approved of Firmage's arrangement—with the exception of four poems, which she rearranged (he recalls that she switched 22 and 27 but does not remember the other two)—and sent it off to the publisher. Manuscript and proofs are now in the Houghton Library collection at Harvard.

It seems strange that Firmage had in mind an order which reverses the one Cummings had in *his* mind, but the fact remains that neither felt very confident about the actual results. And indeed, the book itself shapes up along no very clear sequential lines. It appears to me that the mood in the first fifteen poems is basically positive, that the next three are negative, and that 20–22 are positive again. The next dozen seem mixed, and at the center of the book is a group of very deep sonnets (36–40) dealing with love and death. Following this is a succeeding group of love and mystery poems (41–50), a group of nature poems (51–69), and the final four are mixed but end on a positive note. Except for the central significance of the sonnets, I do not see any other pattern in this sequence.

But I do see a number of significant developments in these poems, nevertheless, and would like to devote the remainder of this chapter to exploring them and relating them to what we have discovered so far about Cummings' life and work from the tales and the photographic captions.

Continuing trends in 95 *Poems* I traced out some years ago, this volume reveals a greater awareness of pain, loss, and emptiness, and a correspondingly greater sense of the difficulty of transcendence.[8] Accepting more of the negative within, the speaker of these poems projects less hatred outward—in accordance with certain trends we will notice in the letters—and there are remarkably few out-and-out satires here. As he feels the ominous threat of annihilation, he becomes more and more concerned with Last Things and comes to terms with death on a level he had not as consistently experienced before. And finally, in matters of technique and style, these poems show an increasing movement toward a hard-won and complex regularity after all those years of experimentation, and an absorption of syntactical, grammatical, and typographic deviations into that accomplished presentational fabric.[9] Over two-thirds of the total are written in Cummings' special way of handling regular stanzaic and sonnet patterns, and the rest are written in his characteristically structured free-verse stanzas. And in terms of diction, he uses less of his tough, dialect-colloquial style on the one hand, and less of his unique conceptual vocabulary on the other, depending therefore mainly on his strong and flexible middle range for speaking of the soberly joyous matters herein.

Let us begin at the bottom of Cummings' seasonal metaphor. In no other book do I recall the emphasis I find here on the dark side of nature—which is often far from the cheerful stoicism of *Adventures in Value*. Number 13 shows the speaker going through a spooky, rainy night, until morning stumbles against his forehead. In 23 we find a creepy midnight scene, where animals and people flicker. Number 41 is another night scene indoors, where clocks speak, and the moon shines through the rain and the wind—"And i and my love are alone." Anguished trees are seen against the sunset in 50. In 54 another tree withstands the shrieking winds of fall. Number 61 shows a snowflake falling on a gravestone.

Then there are those poems presenting failure and ugliness.[10] We find a dirty sunset over the suburbs in 16, and in 17 dogshit mingling with the snow on city streets. In 70 the poet speaks ruefully of artistic failure, and in 51 of the emptiness of a friend's death. But this is not the end of the story, and we see, in 62, the speaker experiencing a bottomless despair from which he nevertheless rises. And it would not be difficult to find in this book, as well as in the preceding ones, many such characteristically affirmative recoveries, wherein the speaker manages to transcend the negative.

But what is really significant in this volume is that, perhaps for the first time, the speaker is presented as experiencing moments during which he accepts and goes into the negative before transcending it. We are shown, uniquely, the *process* involved in transcendence and not just its results. It is not simply a matter, as was the case so often previously, of experiencing the negative, of being aware of it, of acknowledging it, and of then going on to the positive despite that negative; it is rather a question of reaching the positive because of having descended into the negative. It is, in effect, a balancing in the void itself. And most of the poems in this group are among those deep sonnets at the center of the book mentioned above. Number 32 begins:

> all which isn't singing is mere talking
> and all talking's talking to oneself
> (whether that oneself be sought or seeking
> master or disciple sheep or wolf

No matter what we say or how we say it, the poem continues, it is still you (namely I) and nobody else. Then the poem concludes,

> but the very song of(as mountains
> feel and lovers)singing is silence

The carefully balanced use of sing-say-silence occurs many times in 73 *Poems*, and we shall encounter it again before we are done. What is remarkable at this point is the strong note of self-awareness and self-acceptance in the face of negative experience.

In 36 the two lovers are presented as feeling the disappearance of the mortal world at the edge of winter, standing under a star, and experiencing a transcendent acceptance of death: "'dying' the ghost of you / whispers 'is very pleasant' my ghost to." The speaker is going to sleep on a rainy night, in 44, "feeling that sunlight is / (life and day are)only loaned:whereas / night is given(night and death and the rain." In 49 he hears a "tinying" voice at twilight, "a deathless earth's innumerable doom," and feels "acceptance of irrevocable time." The only poem of this kind not a sonnet, number 64 presents a dialogue between the speaker and a purple finch: the former asks why "this summer world . . . must die," and the bird answers, "if i / should tell you anything / . . . i could not sing." Compare the penultimate poem in the book, which reads in its entirety:

> wild(at our first)beasts uttered human words
> —our second coming made stones sing like birds—
> but o the starhushed silence which our third's

But it is in 67 where the full force of experiencing the process of acceptance is felt:

> enter no(silence is the blood whose flesh
> is singing)silence:but unsinging . . .

The speaker is in the abyss between fall and winter, with the spring far beyond:

> . . . and i breathe-move-and-seem some
> perpetually roaming whylessness—
> autumn has gone:will winter never come?

And the speaker utters here one of the most anguished cries to be found in all of Cummings:

> o come,terrible anonymity;enfold
> phantom me with the murdering minus of cold
> —open this ghost with millionary knives of wind—
> scatter his nothing all over what angry skies and . . .

—and—yes, there is a resolution here, but one which gains a hundredfold in intensity from the entering of the pain which has preceded it:

> gently(very whiteness:absolute peace,
> never imaginable mystery)
>   descend[11]

This is indeed "the secret which every mystic tries to tell," but it is even more than that passing "through winter(mystery,dream)" of which Cummings spoke. It is a staying and not just a passing through—for that is the only way of truly passing through. I have spoken elsewhere of how, in 95 *Poems*, Cummings was coming to acknowledge the negative more and learning how to incorporate it into the fabric of his affirmative vision. But what is happening here is that the speaker is going into the negative, and by virtue of its acceptance it becomes part of the affirmation. This, I submit, is a more complex experience and more true to his very concept of transcendence itself. And it does, it seems to me, fulfill certain trends toward true integration we will notice later in the letters: more of the life, in other words, is getting into the poetry, and less is being selected out (more of the life, as I will argue in chapter 5, got into *The Enormous Room* and in *Him*, but his directness in dealing with painful material is much less in evidence in the early and middle poems—partly because poetry is naturally more selective and partly because for some reason he may not have felt entirely ready to try to deal as explicitly with it there).

Thus, when hostile critics dismiss the concept of transcendence as merely one of Cummings' small store of "ideas," the basic point is being entirely missed. What such a poem is actually about is neither the concept of transcendence nor the effective artistic embodiment of that concept; it is rather about the *experience* of self-confrontation, the record of a moment of awareness resulting from taking the ultimate emotional risk—loss of the security-seeking self. One goes through the impasse and accepts the death of a part of the self in the never-ending movement toward growth and integration. Cummings' constant preoccupation with this process is not simply a "theme" of his poetry. It is a lifelong struggle, and his poetry is not only the *record* but also the *instrument* of that struggle. Our job, then, is not to talk about his ideas or how he embodies them. What we should be doing instead is following the process of his struggle within himself, and that can never be reduced to a few clichés about joy, love, spring, the individual, children, and so forth.

Such a struggle is never an easy one, however. And because he was often less than perfect in his awareness, he often dichotomized—both in relation to his art as well as his mind—where he had every intention of integrating. He wrote poems which were dogmatic statements about the necessity of being undogmatic, and he took positions of exclusion even while he was proclaiming harmony and unity. Some of our failings as readers do derive from some of his failures as a writer. Just as he misleads some into saying that his concept of transcendence resembles the "all you need is love" and "just dream your troubles away" mindlessness of Hollywood and Tin Pan Alley, so too does he mislead others into claiming that it involves a separation between the material and the spiritual and the enlightened and the unenlightened.

It seems to me that the basic problem he had difficulty in resolving was whether transcendence meant for him a rising *from* the material *toward* the spiritual, as the Blake reference implies, or whether it meant a rising above the polarities altogether to where there is no difference between the material and the spiritual. In an early essay, Cummings wrote,

> . . . language was not always blest with 'opposites.' Quite the contrary. A certain very wise man has pointed out (in connection with the meaning of dreams) that what 'weak' means and what 'strong' means were once upon a time meant *by one word*. . . .
>
> in burlesk, we meet an echo of the original phenomenon: 'opposites' occur *together*. For that reason, burlesk enables us to (so to speak) *know around* a thing, character, or situation. To put it a little differently: if the art of common-or-garden painting were like the art of burlesk, we should be able to see—impossibly enough—all the way around a solid tree, instead of merely seeing a little more than half of the tree (thanks to binocular parallax or whatever it is) and imagining the rest.[12]

The first sort of transcendence is platonic[13] and lends itself all too well to tension and division, to us against them, and to exclusiveness[14]—although Plato himself varies in his own position, depending upon whether you are reading the "Symposium" or the *Republic*. Cummings' second position, on the other hand, is more truly oriental and encourages integration, harmony, inclusiveness, and acceptance. And evidence for both views can be found in Cummings' writings, although I myself feel it was the second which represented his true commitment. The trouble is, however, that he rarely seemed to notice this fundamental ambiguity in himself and his work, and if he did, he had the devil's own time in dealing with it. Most of the difficulties of his life and work can be traced, I think, to this self-division.

Further indication of such ambiguity is found in several love poems in which this ghostlike, phantom state, where the self is annihilated by nothingness before acceptance results in resolution, is presented as the result of the absence of the lady, which leaves the lover again facing the void:

> your homecoming will be my homecoming—
>
> my selves go with you,only i remain;
> a shadow phantom effigy or seeming (40)

—whose emptiness can be filled, not by traveling the mystic's way down, but only by the beloved's return. And in 47 the lover tells her of his infinite dependency upon her, saying his selves are to her as birds are to the sun:

> without the mercy of
> voice your
> ways (o very most my shining love)
> how more than dark I am, . . .

Compare the conclusion of number 38:

> yours is the light by which my spirit's born:
> yours is the darkness of my soul's return
> —you are my sun,my moon,and all my stars

These are nicely done and are in that courtly tradition Cummings has always managed to carry on so well. But I am forced to conclude that, if he is wholly serious about this (and I am sure he is), he could not quite have realized how contradictory his image of love is in relation to his mystic's vision. It is one thing to fill your emptiness with your own acceptance of nothingness in whose deserts alone can blossom the flowers of rebirth, but it is quite another to fill it with the presence of your beloved. Perhaps this dependency relates back to a certain unresolved ambivalence of his early manhood, which we will examine more closely in chapter 10, in connection with rebelling against yet needing his family and later to his emotional as well as financial need in connection with the Watsons.

On the other hand, it is quite possible that I am being too "platonic" myself in seeing these elements as contradictory. Buddhistic tradition outlines the three essential stages of enlightenment as consisting of materialism, of differentiation, and of reintegration. One who is integrated has achieved a balance between attachment (compassion) and detachment (wisdom): too much of the latter results in quietism and nihilism, while too much of the former leads to sentimentalism and emotionalism. A familiar Zen koan tells the story thus: at first I saw the mountains as mountains and the trees as trees; then I saw that the mountains were not mountains and the trees not trees; now I see that the mountains are mountains and the trees are trees. Although the third stage looks like the first, it is not the same: the first sees nothing spiritual, the second sees the material as symbolizing the spiritual, while the third sees the spiritual *in* the material. The second stage is what happens to people when they first think of enlightenment, distinguishing between good and evil, the enlightened and unenlightened, in order to raise their sights.

In the light of this rather brusque and inadequate summary, then, perhaps we may see Cummings' "contradictions" as representing not so much the clash of opposing visions as the necessary phase of growth between the second and third stages, struggling to balance dependency and independency, love and even-mindedness, hostility and acceptance—a struggle which continues perforce through a series of lifetimes.

Yet the final impression left by 73 *Poems* is of the momentary conclusion of one of those cycles, of intense awareness of Last Things, and of achieved harmony and integration. The speaker reflects in 15 during the early morning between 5 and 6 A.M., hearing some birds and thinking at the stroke of 6:00 that he hears a bell asking "(of / a world born deaf / 'heaven or hell.'" At this hour and in this mood, "civilization" dwindles in the face of reality, and the world is seen balancing unknowingly on the edge of eternity. In 37 lovers experience the presence of the transcendent as a summer night exhibits a falling star: here mystery is revealed, and the intangible is seen as touchable and calculable. Number 39 finds the speaker praying over his sleeping lady that she may encounter the transcendent and return safely:

> faithfully blossoming beyond to breathe
> suns of the night,bring this beautiful
> wanderer home to a dream called time. . . .

And 73, the last poem of this last book, says fittingly, "all worlds have halfsight."[15] They see either with life's eye, which spiritualizes the physical, or with death's, which reduces spirit to materiality. Only love can see the whole, who "strolls the axis of the universe." "Each believing world denies" the half-truth of the other as well as the truth of the whole,

> whereas
> your lover(looking through both life and death)
> timelessly celebrates the merciful
>
> wonder no world deny may or believe

3

Sweepings from the Workbench

:Etcetera: The Unpublished Poems of E. E. Cummings

Written for *SPRING: The Journal of the E. E. Cummings Society* (Old Series) in 1984, this essay continues the account, begun in "Cummings Posthumous," of the poet's work published after his death. The text of *Etcetera*, now included in *Complete Poems 1904–1962* (1991), was originally published in 1983 as part of the Typescript Editions series, edited by George Firmage and Richard Kennedy and issued, under the supervision of Victor Schmalzer, by Liveright, which had become a subdivision of W. W. Norton and primary publisher of Cummings' works.

I

First, let it be said how useful the work is that Richard Kennedy and George Firmage have been doing. Ever since Cummings became a serious subject of book-length studies, and especially since his death, they have contributed significantly to that growing body of scholarly and critical aids which includes by now a collection of his essays, an edition of his letters, bibliographies, biographies, and the like. And here we have a collection of 166 uncollected and unpublished poems, selected from among the more than 350 pieces recovered. This is clearly a valuable addition to Cummingsiana, and I want to explore a few of the areas in which it might prove useful.

Five poems are included which were written when Cummings was ten to eleven years old, and thirteen are included which come from his fourteenth through seventeenth years. Although these have been relegated to the appendices, they are nevertheless striking for their precocious skill, and as such have much to tell us about Cummings' development as a poet. Granted that these poems, along with those at the beginning of the book dating from his Harvard years, when he was seventeen to twenty-two, are piously conventional and "poetic" in metrics, tone, attitude, subject, and style, they nonetheless reveal a youngster who has committed his life to his craft, and who is working diligently to master that craft. His way was logically to absorb the late Victorian and Edwardian atmosphere around him, and then to work back through the nineteenth century to its romantic and Victorian sources.

By 1916, however, as the editors point out, when he was twenty-two, his encounter with modernism was beginning to make itself felt in his writing. And the fact that this encounter coincided exactly with his own personal liberation from the comfortable Cambridge and Harvard which had nourished him is not without its special significance, for just as logically he had now to find new forms and styles for new feelings and experiences. Yet he still continued to be a meticulous craftsman, and the poems he wrote as a maturing and mature poet are just as carefully done as those he wrote as a conventional youngster, for he undertook his exercises in experimentation with as much systematic zeal as he had previously done in mastering the traditional stanzas.

This truth has never been fully appreciated in many of the reviews or in much of the criticism, although most serious students of Cummings have always known it. Perhaps Cummings himself, with his frequent thematic emphasis on spontaneity and feeling as opposed to systematic thought and intellect, encouraged readers to assume his poems, and particularly his typographical experiments, were free, casual, and slapdash. Such a misconception has too often been accompanied by a corollary—that he simply published everything he ever wrote—which misconception this volume as conclusively disproves as the other.

But *does* this systematic approach to his craft belie Cummings' consistent emphasis on his spontaneity theme? I think not, and here is a further misconception which I myself have taken—and am still taking—some trouble to counteract. Cummings' point is, and always was, that spontaneity requires a great deal of effort, and anyone who has mastered a difficult skill in order to win an effortless ease can readily understand what this process means. Even in the realm of the self and not just in the realm of craft or art, it takes a great deal of effort to cut oneself away from one's shaping influences, as Cummings did from Cambridge and Harvard, to stand forth as a whole and independent individual. And yet one makes a self out of the materials that were given, reworking them, it may be, and even adding somewhat, but never wholly otherwise. Thus the skillful if tame regularities of Cummings' youthful poems remain to inform the most original and daring experiments of his mature years.

But the opposite is equally true: the more original aspects of his mature art were sometimes anticipated by his immature work, and we realize he was an individual all along. Thus, even in his early, premodernist college poems an occasional anticipation of his later and more characteristic voice is heard: "The air is strange with rare birds after rain"; "whose most white body is his voice. / Night shall eat these girls and boys"; "To barter day and thought for night and ecstasy"; "In that how little hand"; "frail candles . . . total terror of the actual dark / Changing the shy equivalents of dream"; "irrevocable mountains"; "the probable stars"; "perpendicular odors"; "the swiftly singular / Adventure of one inadvertent star"; "Working angels / Shovel light in heaven / . . . God drives the jingling world"; etc.

On the other hand, I do not find any lost masterpieces among the mature selections included here from the unpublished and uncollected poems. With a small number of exceptions, he does nothing here that he does not do better in his published work; poem after poem struggles to organize itself around the familiar brilliance of Cummings' unique art, and time after time a lame phrase or a trite image defeats that struggle. Nor do these poems evince the full maturing vision of life which to me is the raison d'être of his career, although the editors seem to see here more than I. Perhaps there is a message in all this: that a poet's skill in his craft remains merely craft until he finds what he feels he needs to express. And that craft has its limits when left to its own devices. Cummings was well advised not to worry about publishing or collecting these poems.

II

Can anything further be said, then, in favor of the wisdom of publishing and collecting them thus in book form? I think it can. A chief use of this book would be to match up poems here with those in the already published volumes on similar subjects and from the same time period, and thereby to study the differences for Cummings between artistic failure and success. The comparison would reveal a lot about his artistic success. For example, on page 37 of *Etcetera* is a different typographical version of "the / sky / was / can dy lu / minous," which appeared in its canonical form at the beginning of *XLI Poems* (1925), and an analysis of the changes should prove rewarding. As with the publication of *The Waste Land* manuscript, for example, or J. W. Beach's study of Auden's revisions, or with any set of poetic worksheets, we can tell much about the final version of a work by discovering what was left out or rearranged or recomposed.

Sweepings from the poet's workbench, then, but valuable nevertheless. As for the exceptions I referred to, one that stands out for me is entitled "BALLADE" and is on page 156, coming from the latter portion of the selection called "LATE POEMS, 1930–62" (there's no indication of whether its five sections are divided chronologically). In each of the three major stanzas the speaker confronts a different horror—a drunken bum lying on a "bowery / dump's filthy floor," a black man hanging from an executioner's rope, and the man who dropped the atom bomb over Japan—and in each case the speaker disclaims any superiority, "because," as he says, "the poor sonofabitch is i." The brief fourth stanza concludes with him identifying in turn with the "illimitable Mystery / whom worlds must always crucify," and asserting once again "because the poor sonofabitch is i."

What strikes me here is the unalloyed compassion and the sense conveyed by the speaker of his own implication in the suffering, failures, and mistakes of others. We recall a similar compassion, of course, in many of Cummings' published works, and yet we might also recall that it comes characteristically mixed in (and mixed up) with a prideful sense of difference separating the speaker and those he identifies with from soulless "mostpeople." In "a man who had fallen among thieves" (*is* 5, XXVIII), for example, the speaker contrasts his tenderness toward the victim with the indifference of "a dozen staunch and leal / citizens" who pause and then turn away in disgust. This you-and-me-against-the-world mood is one of Cummings' least appealing attitudes, and my guess is that it accounts for more of the hostility he too often provokes in potentially sympathetic readers than all his technical and linguistic experiments put together.

Possibly apart from the fourth stanza, which almost drags the poem back into a me-and-Christ-against-the-world stance, and which therefore may be why he elected not to publish it, this "BALLADE" sounds a fuller note toward which the mature Cummings was evolving before he died and which promised to transcend an already brilliant achievement.

4

Hopkins, Cummings, and the Struggle of the Modern

This chapter was originally written at the request of Richard Giles, who was compiling in 1985 a book of essays on Gerard Manley Hopkins and his influence on the moderns. It became an interesting occasion for me to approach the relationship of Cummings to modernism from a somewhat different angle than in chapter 1.

I

I have found no direct evidence that Cummings was actually influenced by Hopkins, and indeed it may be that he did not even *like* Hopkins. Nevertheless, a significant number of critics over the years, beginning at least as early as Gardner's first volume in 1944,[1] have seen fit to compare them. And that comparison is, of course, related to the whole question of modernism in poetry and all that it implies. I too believe there are instructive similarities between the two poets, even though we must consider these similarities as parallels rather than as matters of influence, for the true importance of the similarities lies in certain common temperamental responses to a common influence. If we consider these writers in terms of the question of modernism, then, I would hope that a small but meaningful piece of the literary history of the past several hundred years will seem a bit clearer as a result.

As we know, after Hopkins was published posthumously in 1918, and especially after the second edition in 1930, he was hailed as a forerunner and kindred spirit by many modernist poets and critics. Because he was also obviously very much a man of his own time, however, others developed a minority tradition of seeing him as a Victorian, and more have recently followed suit in decrying the whole modernization of the nineteenth century and reaffirming the Victorianism of Victorian literature. But I do not think such polarization is very helpful, and it is as futile to say the Victorians are not modern as it used to be to say the moderns were anti-Victorian. The most promising trend, it seems to me, is that more comprehensive one which says, yes, Hopkins was a Victorian, but the Victorians anticipated modernism in many ways, in that they and we have been facing similar problems and struggling with similar adaptations—that, as a matter of fact, this struggle began with the Romantics.

This third tradition is as aware of the differences between the nineteenth and twentieth centuries as the other two traditions, but it regards them as differences of degree and not of kind. Thus, the Victorians confronted the abyss but did not go into it; they felt ambivalent about the self but were convinced there was such a thing; they feared the darker aspects of nature but did not sever all connection with it. Similarly, when it comes to experimental forms for encompassing shifts in consciousness, they evolved dramatized lyrics but did not fully yield to a relativist or perspectivist position; they tried lyricizing drama and epic but did not entirely succeed in exploring the depths of the mind; they risked introducing "non-" or "anti-Victorian" subject matter into the lyric but did not really free themselves of conventional moral restrictions. In this way, we can see more easily what it is reasonable to expect: that, having preceded us on those frontiers, they could not have been as familiar with or feel as at home in certain territories as we are. The map is the same, only ours has by now become more detailed. To be sure, any number of lesser Victorians can be found, and even portions of the major poets, who do not fit this description, but certainly the same can be said for some moderns. A period concept is not determinative of all that can be found within certain chronological boundaries; it is an attempt, rather, to bring into view what appears to be of dominant significance there.

Todd Bender provides the most convincing argument I have seen which views Hopkins from this point of view,[2] although Gardner's monumental study can be said to have anticipated it. Far from being the bold "original" or unknowing sport of time he has often been taken to be, Hopkins was in tune with the protomodernist tendencies of his age, as well as with influences from his close study of classical literature, theological texts, and metaphysical poetry. To this list we may add the Victorian nonsense poets[3] and the oft-noted interest Hopkins showed in Anglo-Saxon and Welsh poetry. Perhaps the sole protomodernist tendency whose influence Hopkins does *not* show is French symbolism, and for that he in all probability died too soon.

Cummings' position vis-à-vis modernism, as we have seen in chapter 1, has also been a disputed one. Hailed early on as a radical experimenter and avant-garde poet, he was later condemned as a nineteenth-century sentimentalist who used linguistic and typographical tricks to disguise that fact. Indeed, the paradox is that, if the poetry of self-doubt and inner conflict we have inherited from the nineteenth century be taken as characteristic of modernism, then Hopkins could be seen as *more* modern than Cummings. I hope, however, that a juster estimate of Cummings' place in twentieth-century poetry is in the making and that we can briefly suggest its outlines here.

II

Keeping these distinctions in mind, let us now look a bit more closely at how our two poets are alike and unlike. What immediately confronts the eye is that both are strikingly intense lyric poets—along with the narrowness which such intensity can imply—often given to writing unconventional sonnets, and characteristically moved to unusual joy by the vision of nature. Also obvious is that both are deliberate, persistent, extravagant, and painstaking innovators, inventors, experimentalists. As we explore their careers a bit further, we find that both were influenced by classical literature and nineteenth-century aestheticism; both were inveterate, compulsive, and microscopic journal and notebook writers; and both were keenly interested in painting and music. Clearly different, however, are Hopkins' religious as opposed to Cummings' artistic vocation, and the former's later mood of despair as opposed to Cummings' basic affirmativeness. Additionally, Cummings' satires, sex and love poems, and interest in the city and the demimonde find no parallel in Hopkins.

Their closest point of contact is in their eccentric stylistic experiments. Both regarded words as tangible objects and were obsessed by their look and sound and feel; both strove for a fresh, mixed, natural, and dramatic style; both strained the bounds of syntax to the limit and beyond; both indulged in grammatical shifts, the splitting and interweaving of words, and the roughing up of rhythm; and both are often dense, compact, ambiguous, difficult. An important difference is Hopkins' reliance on the ear as opposed to Cummings' on the eye—although Babette Deutsch finds that Cummings' typographical displacements attempt to do visually what Hopkins did by means of his peculiarities of diction, to present the inscape of *things*,[4] while John Press says that Cummings' visuality does what Hopkins aimed at with his notation system, to attain a new degree of poetic accuracy.[5]

Even more important, though, is their common concern with developing the nonlogical structure of poems, for this is where they touch upon the question of modernism even more closely. Bender has shown how, in studying Pindar, Hopkins arrived at a theory sounding very much like the Romantics' associative and organic form principle, Herbert Read's collage effect, Ford Madox Ford's unearned increment, Ransom's texture and structure, etc. Hopkins seized upon the idea that a poem could be organized by a pattern of images, connotations, and feelings, in addition to or instead of a sequence of thoughts and actions, and he knew that for what he had to express it was the best embodiment. Cummings, too, having behind him the further experiments of the symbolists and cubists, as a young man developed the possibilities of fragmentation, juxtaposition, and montage for poetry—which in part explains his concern over typography—and also feeling that what he had to express was best put in that way. And that expression, in both cases, was an extension of the metaphoric principle, effectively to put disparate experiences together so as to create a new meaning.

So the key issue behind all such experimentation is to define what this new meaning is. It is generally agreed that the major artistic shift of the past two hundred years has been away from an attempt to represent the world and toward an attempt to represent the inner self responding to that world and struggling to forge a humane consciousness suitable to increasingly technological conditions. The form of the poem must follow the contours of that inner experience. The poetry of logic and narrative, then, is a poetry of product, while the poetry of metaphor is of process; in the former, poetry is a criticism of life, while in the latter it is an exploration of life. The first requirement of the poetry of process is that it *participate* in the struggle of the self with the world: it must look and feel like an experience, and it must not fall into a detachable content wrapped up in a decorative form. The second requirement is that it press the reader to *participate in the poem*, even as the poem participates in experience, so that the reader will not be able to extract a paraphrasable meaning or deal with a substitute for the experience of the poem itself. Thus, whatever devices can be discovered which will make for immediacy, abruptness, concreteness, dramatic urgency, simultaneity, evocativeness, irreducibility, allusiveness, suggestiveness, multiplicity of overlapping perspectives and meanings—syntactic, grammatical, and dictional shifts, typographical displacements, bending of rhythmic patterns, associative rather than logical or narrative structures—these will be energetically deployed in the service of striving for this difficult balance.

III

Now, while these are the general defining characteristics of modernism, and of its antecedents in the nineteenth century, they apply to Hopkins and Cummings in a special way. If most modernists dislocated linguistic and structural conventions, Hopkins and Cummings did so in a way peculiar to themselves. Their twisting of grammar and syntax far exceeds that of most modernists (Stein and Joyce excepted), their handling of the metaphoric principle has been much more concentrated on the lyric than that of most modernists, and their effort to achieve a unity of vision has been much more focused on the intuition of immanence as opposed to the existential sense of alienation than that of most modernists (Joyce, Stevens, and Williams come to mind as exceptions).

Hillis Miller has shown how Hopkins struggled to sustain a vision of monism in the face of long centuries of the dualistic tradition.[6] An immanent God allows one to feel that "being and value lie in *this* world, in what is immediate, tangible, present to man, in earth, sun, sea, in the stars in their courses, and in what Yeats was to call 'the foul rag-and-bone shop of the heart.'"[7] An absent God, on the other hand, makes one feel uncomfortable with this world and long to be united with a deity who has withdrawn Himself from it. Cummings also, as I've shown in chapter 2, largely on a more secular plane, struggled with his own ambivalence over whether he was following Lao-tzu or Plato—and if Plato, whether of the "Symposium" or the *Republic*—but in his best moments he remained true to his own credo: "never to rest and never to have:only to grow. / Always the beautiful answer who asks a more beautiful question."[8] And a line from Hopkins' journals sounds almost as if it comes straight out of Cummings: "nothing is so pregnant and straightforward to the truth as simple *yes* and *is*."[9] If the most spiritual significance resides in the most tangible representation, and if we cannot do justice to one without the other, then the poetry of monism must be complex, organic, and dramatic.

A poem must follow the contours of experience, then, but not just of any experience. The experience of immanence is achieved by acceptance of and submission to the natural conditions of existence. It is therefore an experience, in the first place, of integration, reconciliation, simultaneity, both/and versus either/or. It is correspondingly an experience, in the second place, of process, of being *in* the unfolding of natural life, of motion, of constantly changing and evolving understandings. And it is consequently an experience, in the third place, of the struggle to surrender dualism, for which the human mind has a well-nigh irresistible urge, and thus it may involve periods of emptiness, descent, and despair as the mind discovers it can no longer hold onto dualism yet cannot accept and submit to the natural conditions of reality. It is finally an experience of lyric intensity, calling for linguistic and structural innovations simply to *begin* doing justice to its force. The traditions of immanence are at least as ancient as those of dualism, perhaps more so, but for our purpose they were being rediscovered or reinvented in a steady line from Blake, through Hallam's essay on Tennyson, to Browning, Whitman, and Meredith, and up to Yeats' "A Dialogue of Self and Soul" (which presents a perfect paradigm of the struggle between the two traditions). It is as significant members of this line that Hopkins and Cummings achieve their true importance.

IV

Thus, as Hopkins had his development from joyful-sensuous-flamboyant to serious-spiritual-muted poems, so too did Cummings develop similarly. In the second half of his career, as we have seen, he became less interested in sex and satire—where his fear often projected itself outward—and more concerned with love, despair, and death. There is even a group of "terrible sonnets," as we have seen, in the posthumous 73 *Poems*. And the early experiments for both poets became later mastery as they achieved—if not victory over their inner conflict—at least a strong and flexible form for embodying it organically.

If the "recovery of immanence" is "the inner drama of twentieth-century literature," as Miller claims,[10] or one main part of that drama, as I would rather say, then both Hopkins and Cummings left behind a living record of the struggle to achieve this recovery, and both invented artistic forms for doing so. If this definition allows us to see Cummings as a true modernist, as well as to view Hopkins in the actual context of his age, it also allows us to see both as developing aspects of a single, still evolving phase of literary history.

5

The Two Cummingses

:A Reconsideration

Previously unpublished, the papers comprising this chapter were originally presented as talks at the American Literature Association's conferences in 1991 and 1992. Although delivered thus separately, they were conceived as a unit and so are combined here. My concern of late has been to aim at a balanced assessment of Cummings' powers and limitations — an enterprise begun in chapter 2 and continuing below in chapters 10, 12, and 14. My intent is to try to sort out what is most alive and enduring from what seems, in retrospect, less valuable. I begin with the problem of defining the latter.

I

Negative criticism of Cummings' vision falls into two camps: either his view of life is not to be taken seriously; or it *is*, but he somehow doesn't fulfill its promise. While doing what I can to counter the first, I now begin to move toward examining more fully the second.

There is no question in my mind about a transcendental-organicist vision: it a valid position, with ancient roots, deeply influencing much of the best thought and art of the past two centuries. But even Cummings himself saw, as Richard Kennedy's biography shows, some unresolved inner conflict as frustrating his efforts at remaining true to this vision and at writing significant longer works. His growth was somewhat impeded by an ambivalence which he too seldom seemed to want or be able either to confront or incorporate into his art.

He seems at times to be taking away with one hand what he gives with the other, as if there were two poets within—one a poet of experience and the other a moralist—who often had difficulty in coming to terms with one another. The result is a curious reversal of values underlying some of the work in a rather contradictory way. I shall try here to separate them out so as to place what I take to be his true genius on a firmer basis.

1.

The problem can be usefully approached at the start from the perspective of the unacknowledged and unassimilated conflict found in the introduction to the 1938 *Collected Poems*, almost at the midpoint of his career. The difficulty is that, after having divided humankind into "mostpeople" (snobs) and "you and I" (human beings), Cummings concludes with a rapturous affirmation of the transcendence of division: "Never the murdered finalities of wherewhen and yesno,impotent nongames of wrongright and rightwrong," and so on.

The trouble here, of course, is that he derives his denial of categories from out of the prior establishment of categories. But a truly transcendental vision, as in Whitman, for example, is inclusive, and if it sees "mostpeople" as enslaved by habit and routine, it nevertheless identifies with and accepts their humanity in the common struggle to retain some vitality in the face of trying to meet life's essential obligations and responsibilities.

But there is a tendency among certain transcendentalists—Thoreau is another example—to become snappish. It is one thing to reject the encroaching sterility of our bourgeois/commercial/technological society, but it is quite another to hold oneself aloof from the necessary processes of life itself. Is there not, after all, a fatal gap in Thoreau's self-assigned task of stripping life down to its essentials, in that he neglects to confront the very *basis* of human existence —the imperative to mate and beget and nurture children, and all that it implies?

What too often happens upon the failure to understand this distinction is the defiant adoption of the stance of the rebellious artist, beneath which is perhaps a fear of not being accepted as one is and the defensive gesture of rejecting *before* being rejected. This ambivalence is matched, as we have seen, by a parallel ambiguity in the concept of "transcendence" itself, which can mean opposite things: on the one hand, it refers to what is *beyond* material existence, and thus it stands in opposition to "immanence" as referring to what is *within* the limits of possible experience; and on the other, it refers to the notion that spirit resides *within* matter, thus it runs parallel to "immanence" as referring to the indwelling presence of God in the world. The first meanings imply a dualistic view of the universe, while the second suggest a nondualistic view, and Cummings was not always clear about where he stood in *this* matter. When one follows the dualistic line, one can easily become enmeshed in categorizing, the you-and-me-against-mostpeople polarity, whereas when one takes the nondualistic approach, one tends to see, with Blake, for example, eternity in a grain of sand, and to proclaim that everything that lives is holy. But of course these problems did not simply come out of Cummings' head: they were a result also of his particular life experience and of his times.

2.

As we shall see in greater detail in chapters 10 and 12, there is first the matter of his early relationship with his parents. His mother was a warm, accepting, and encouraging presence—perhaps a little too much so—while his father was an imposing and in some ways a forbidding one. Although Cummings took pains to praise his father in public, in private he was much more ambivalent. Without more than hinting at the obvious oedipal problems, we can point out that while the father was an active, successful, and socially involved figure, Cummings grew to dislike reformers and do-gooders and to take pride in standing apart from society.

But a number of traumatic events occurred during what I shall call the Crucial Decade between 1917 and 1927, when he was twenty-three to thirty-three years of age, to complicate his feelings about his father. As we know, during the early days of the First World War, Cummings spent the better part of three months in a French detention facility under quite primitive conditions during the latter portion of 1917. The defiantly idealistic young poet went through a very difficult ordeal, and much the worse for wear, he was finally released through the frantic efforts of his father before the situation could deteriorate further.

The Enormous Room (1922) was, of course, his first published book, and he wrote it at his father's urging. Its *message*, however, was anti-establishment, anti-authoritarian, and pro-individual—the more alienated and seedy, the better.

3.

Soon after his release in January 1918, he fell in love with Elaine Orr Thayer, whose marriage to Cummings' Harvard classmate Scofield Thayer was beginning to dissolve, and she and Cummings became romantically involved. Their daughter Nancy was born in 1919, Elaine and Thayer were divorced in 1921, and she and Cummings were married in 1924, but the relationship foundered during that same year; Elaine remarried shortly thereafter, and Cummings' connection with his five-year-old daughter, who was subsequently raised without knowing he was her father, was effectively suspended. Here again he turned to his father for help and hoped to gain some sort of visitation rights, but their efforts failed. In 1926, Edward Cummings Sr. died in a tragic auto accident.

We can see Cummings struggling with the interwoven issues of his marriage, the imminent birth of a child, the problem of the dedicated artist as husband and father-to-be, the specter of "mostpeople," and the countervailing release provided by the circus, vaudeville, burlesque, and bawdry in his play *Him* of 1927. This work represents Cummings at his best, in my opinion, for he portrays the wife's point of view as sensitively and sympathetically as his own, however limited it may seem from a more recent feminist perspective.[1] And whereas Cummings rarely reveals in his published works any doubts or second thoughts, here he gives them full and dramatic play.

What we have seen, then, is a brilliant young artist starting out, with every self-confidence, along the path to early adulthood, getting hit by a series of severe blows to his physical and mental health, and pausing to confront and work it all out in literary form. But it is what happens afterward that is quite puzzling.

4.

He was in psychoanalysis during 1928–29, went to Russia in 1931, and met Marion Morehouse in 1932. The upshot was, as his 1932 introduction to the Modern Library edition of *The Enormous Room* shows, that he believed artists were more important than mostpeople: "I feel [people who don't become artists] don't become: I feel nothing happens to them; I feel negation becomes of them." The dialogue form is being used here much less dramatically than in his play, and we are well on our way to the above-mentioned introduction of the 1938 *Collected Poems*. We are also seeing that defensive reaction of the modernist artist against the emerging social consciousness of the thirties.

What ensued is consistent, as we shall examine in chapter 12, with these developments. The adult Nancy, when she was 27, having learned by now that Cummings was once married to her mother, came to meet him in 1946. They became friends and, a few years later, as he was painting her portrait, he revealed himself to her as her natural father. She was delighted and asked him to take on his role as grandfather to her own children. Although, as Kennedy's biography shows, Cummings began questioning his whole artistic project under the stress of this request, he finally could not find it within himself to alter his style of life by then, rejecting outright any infringement upon his freedom to devote the bulk of his time to his arts. And it is certainly heartbreaking that, during the same year in which Nancy came to him, he published his verse play *Santa Claus*, wherein a young daughter is shown searching for her lost father and having a long-sought reconciliation with him.

Here is a highly defended ego boundary and the compensatory need to be strict about who and what one will include and exclude in order to feel safe. Such defensiveness ties in very well with the difficulty of separating from an overly close bond with one's mother and an ambivalence over the too-insistent need to assert one's individuality in the face of the fear of engulfment. In this case, we can add his rejection *and* need of the father he had lost in the midst of his Crucial Decade. Hence Cummings' urge *publicly* to praise his father as well as the ostensibly idyllic home life of his childhood—which we also find, interestingly enough, in his sister's autobiography, discussed below in chapter 13.

5.

The same ambivalence crops up again in what at first appears to be a retraction twenty-one years later of his original point about the supremacy of art. (And I find I'm confronting my *own* ambivalence here, contradicting the interpretation of this passage I published thirty years ago!)[2] At the conclusion of Nonlecture Five, which, significantly, deals with his play called *Him*, he is finally able to say, "we should go hugely astray in assuming that art was the only true selftranscendence. Art is a mystery; all mysteries have their source in a mystery-of-mysteries who is love." But then he leaves an escape hatch open: "and if lovers may reach eternity directly through love herself, their mystery remains essentially that of the loving artist whose way must lie through his art, and of the loving worshipper whose aim is oneness with god."

What seems like an acknowledgment of the primacy of human relationship *over* art turns out to be a more subtle way of re-asserting the primacy of *art*. And he does this by means of another sleight-of-hand with categories, attaching "loving" to both art and religion. He seems to be saying, that is, that although love is the direct path to self-transcendence, art and religion are equal paths, however indirect. But in what sense can we say that "the loving artist" and "the loving worshipper" are equivalent to "lovers," who are in touch with the "source" of "all mysteries," the "mystery of mysteries who is love"? Are these in fact simply alternative ways of loving, and do we really have a choice?

If we look at *Him* itself, we'll see portrayed the struggle of the artist to unite his vocation with his role as husband and father-to-be, and the dramatic outcome is Him's "cry of terror" at the sight of Me holding in her arms "a newborn babe." The implication seems clear that the two needs *should* be united. In his correspondence with me on this question of their disharmony, quoted in my *E. E. Cummings: The Growth of a Writer* (58), Cummings explains: "He loves,not herself,but the loveliness of his mistress;she loves,not himself,but the possibility of making a husband out of a lover." The equations are clear so far: lover-and-mistress/husband-and-wife are false roles covering up the true inner selves of each—herself/himself.

Somewhat earlier, Him and Me are having their last real talk, and this is what he concludes:

> In all directions I cannot move. Through you I have made a discovery: you have shown me something . . . something about which I am doubtful deep in my heart. I cannot feel that everything has been a mistake— that I have inhabited an illusion with you merely to escape from reality and the knowledge of ourselves. (*To himself*) How should what is desirable shut us entirely from what is? No! That must not be quite all: I will not think that the tragedy can be so simple. There must be something else: I believe there IS something else: and my heart tells me that unless I discover this now I will never discover it.—Am I wrong?

Him has previously identified the desirable, in Keatsian terms, with Beauty, and what is—what exists—with Truth, and he has said that "beauty has shut me from truth."

Now the whole art of the play has been deployed to conceal-while-revealing the fact that Me is pregnant but is unwilling to use that fact to bind her distracted lover more securely to herself. What we have here is an enormously complex set of circumstances, and they inevitably reflect what was going on in Cummings' life at the time: the "secret" birth of his and Elaine's child, their tenuous relationship, his loss of her and the child, his new union with Anne Barton, whose quote serves as the epigraph to the published edition of this play, and so forth. It seems that Cummings was thrown into a profound dilemma about the relationship between his human and artistic commitments, a dilemma which he confronted once again twenty or so years later when the grown child appeared and he was writing another play about the same issue—that is, *Santa Claus.*

And I believe that he knew—although confiding it only to his notebooks—that his difficulties in holding onto that child signified that he—*and* his art—were missing something terribly important. The solution, then, to the problem of false roles and the consequent polarizing of roles would seem to reside in the appearance of the child as a third or reconciling term, the transcendent epiphany of mother-giving-birth/father-loving-both, the resolution of the Beauty/Truth dilemma. Thus do their true inner selves meet to produce their issue, which in turn symbolizes their transcendence of self. The problem then becomes the fact that Cummings seems to assign varying meanings to "selftranscendence": it means—or should mean—on the one hand, the transcendence of roles and the ability to make true contact with another; but it also means, on the other hand, one's uniqueness, the individuality which one does *not* share with anyone else. Paradoxically, then, "love" means finding one's true self, apart from all other selves, and at the same time, we may infer, finding someone who will selflessly recognize, appreciate, and support that self—somewhat in the fashion of a good-enough mother—without the danger of engulfment and loss of boundaries.

But love and selfhood—as with art and religion—simply cannot be conflated like this. It is as if he were saying that, to be *able* to love, one needs first to *be* loved—which is, significantly, more appropriate between mother and child than adult lovers. Cummings typically reveals his compulsive need to patrol the boundaries even in the midst of trying to "transcend" them.

6.

After the stressful years of his young manhood, then, Cummings seems to have decided that it was no longer permissible to publish his doubts about himself, for it was apparently his defensive rationalization that the artist must present a consistent face to his public. The real loss is not that he was incapable of self-examination and self-criticism—for his psychoanalysis and his notebooks amply demonstrate the contrary—but rather that he made some sort of self-protective decision to keep that side of himself *to* himself. The result is, as I've suggested, that he gives with one hand and takes away with the other. We are to celebrate love, acceptance, and natural process, but we are not to accept or love those who have difficulty with that task. We are to love and live our lives fully, but we are not to take responsibility for personally supporting the ground of our literal existence in the world.

We may agree that a poet of experience, even though he expresses willy-nilly a vision of life, has no responsibility other than to be true to the moment; he need not strive for a foolish consistency, nor need he succumb to the temptation to generalize. We read him for what he is worth as a privileged conveyer of how life looks and feels to him as he is living it. A moralist, on the other hand, must either practice what he preaches or be willing to share with us our common human imperfections. The authentic moralist cannot scorn the necessity of making a living while at the same time begging his wealthy friends for funds.

He didn't seem to realize how contradictory it was to focus so insistently on themes of authenticity and openness while at the same time keeping half of his true self hidden. He really wanted to go in one direction, but his unresolved inner struggle kept pulling him in the other. Leaving out of his published writings his fear of engulfment and the consequent self-doubts about his entire life-project resulted in their being projected outward and expressed in such a way as to contradict those very professions of openness, confidence, and acceptance.

Indeed, the conflict often shows up in the very structure of his poems themselves, most typically in love poems where, while he is praising his lady and exalting their love, he is simultaneously derogating mostpeople because they don't know how to love as successfully. Thus what he would most passionately believe in is undermined by a contradictory exclusiveness—a bravado very much like Hemingway's, whose pretensions about *his* inner circle of aficionados Cummings so wittily punctured in his epigrammatic satire on the novelist (*No Thanks*, #26). He also cautioned Pound in private correspondence, as we shall see, against excessive virulence in satire. Who will judge the judges?

7.

I do not close my case here, however. As I have said, these remarks are intended as a preliminary to locating where his true genius as a poet of experience lies. I believe that much of the modernist enterprise as a whole is afflicted by a similar struggle between art and life, and that Cummings is representative of his age. But the best of Cummings is to be found in those moments of pure vision, joy, and love, all the more precious for what they cost him, and in those flashes of satire where he hits accurately at our follies without needing to exempt himself.

II

We turn now, therefore, to examine what sort of poetry Cummings could write when not entangled in the coils of his own rarely acknowledged ambivalence and defensive self-protectiveness.

I see the issue in terms of points along a spectrum. On the left side are the satires, and on the right are the celebrations, with the varying mixtures coming in between. Thus, I begin with those satires which, although they *are* polarized between good and evil, do *not* rest upon the assumed difference between good-poet versus bad-others, nor amount to personal self-justification at the expense of mostpeople.

1.

The first one is #32 from *73 Poems* (1963):

> all which isn't singing is mere talking
> and all talking's talking to oneself
> (whether that oneself be sought or seeking
> master or disciple sheep or wolf)
>
> gush to it as deity or devil
> —toss in sobs and reasons threats and smiles
> name it cruel fair or blessed evil—
> it is you(né i)nobody else

> drive dumb mankind dizzy with haranguing
> —you are deafened every mother's son—
> all is merely talk which isn't singing
> and all talking's to oneself alone
>
> but the very song of(as mountains
> feel and lovers)singing is silence

The object of satire here, of course, is "talking," but this implies, further, a polarized sort of search for "oneself"—"deity or devil"—or even an oxymoronic "cruel fair or blessed evil." But we never find it—and notice how the speaker includes himself—for talking doesn't get us anywhere. It only makes us dizzy, it just deafens us, and it is merely a self-referring and lonely business. Then the alternative is brought in: "but the very song of singing is silence." Not only does this contrast with talking, it also intensifies the contrast in being the *essence* of singing—which opens out the implications faster than it closes them up. We find *ourselves* when we *stop* talking, abandon polarities and oxymorons, and rest in the paradox of the silent song. The polarities are transcended.

This is among Cummings' best sonnets, experimental without being excessively distorted, formal without being rigidly regular.

2.

The next point along the spectrum includes those satires which are actually *compassionate* in their highlighting of mankind's and society's follies and shortcomings, and this leads to a softening of the polarity, to less anger and scorn, and to more of a sense of pity and concern—which is, of course, even less a matter of me-versus-mostpeople than we may find in the first group.

This is the familiar #8 from "New Poems," in *Collected Poems* (1938):

> this little bride & groom are
> standing)in a kind
> of crown he dressed
> in black candy she
>
> veiled with candy white
> carrying a bouquet of
> pretend flowers this
> candy crown with this candy

> little bride & little
> groom in it kind of stands on
> a thin ring which stands on a much
> less thin very much more
>
> big & kinder of ring & which
> kinder of stands on a
> much more than very much
> biggest & thickest & kindest
>
> of ring & all one two three rings
> are cake & everything is protected by
> cellophane against anything(because
> nothing really exists

The object of satire here is the unreality of the conventional wrapping in which we encapsulate love, sex, and relationship, and the imagery, diction, rhythm, and structure all perfectly conspire to suggest—rather than state—the theme, so that, by the end, only the barest flick of the pen is required to point it up. The slight suggestion of baby talk, the incremental buildup, the lack of punctuation, the run-on lines, the placing of the reverse parentheses—all encase the poem verbally as the cellophane encases the bride and the groom physically, and we are to understand that there isn't much difference between these candy figurines and the actual bride and groom of the wedding itself.

Thus the poem as a whole rests upon the intertwined correspondences among the threefold layers of the cake, the threefold removal from reality of the experience of love—real love, conventional love, figurine love—and the threefold structure of the poem—figurines/cake/cellophane. And it is all done, at least as it seems to me, without self-righteous bitterness.

3.

We move now toward celebrations, and first on the way are those poems which, although they *do* include negatives to contrast with and reinforce the positives, do it, as in the first group of satires, without the me-against-them polarity or the need for personal self-justification.

The poem I've chosen is #42 from 50 *Poems* (1940):

> love is more thicker than forget
> more thinner than recall
> more seldom than a wave is wet
> more frequent than to fail

it is most mad and moonly
and less it shall unbe
than all the sea which only
is deeper than the sea

love is less always than to win
less never than alive
less bigger than the least begin
less littler than forgive

it is most sane and sunly
and more it cannot die
than all the sky which only
is higher than the sky

The first three stanzas engage us in a series of reverse polarities, intertwined with a series of abstractions being treated in terms of concrete qualities—almost personifications but certainly some kind of metaphor. The object of praise is, of course, love, and the strategy is to establish a series of contrasts where one thing is "more" than another. Love is thicker than forget, thinner than recall, "*more* thicker" and "*more* thinner" creating a further complication with the double comparative. "Forget" must be pretty thick if love is to be intensified by being thicker, "recall" must be very thin if love is to be thinner, the point being that love is both *very* thick and *very* thin—that is, beyond, above, outside the categories—transcendent: "it is most mad and moonly."

The rest of the poem rings the changes on this theme. Notice the rhyming quatrains, the repetition-and-variation of "it is most sane and sunly," and so on, all of which helps to create that effect of moving into and out of opposites, a soft-shoe shuffle, a sleight-of-hand. The function of the polarities here is to express the inexpressible, rather than to contrast you-and-I with mostpeople, a task which Cummings carries off with remarkable effectiveness, and which his unique stylistic innovations are especially suited to accomplish.

4.

The next step along the spectrum toward pure acceptance includes those poems which, although they too include the negative, do so in such a way as to transcend it—by going *into* and *through* it—a structural feature much favored by the New Critics of that period. But where *they* spoke of holding opposites in tension, as we have seen, *Cummings'* strategy involves an *inte-*

gration of the negative *into* the positive, so that the latter arises *out of* the former. This poem is #49 of *No Thanks* (1935):

> silent unday by silently not night
>
> did the great world(in darkly taking rain)
> drown,beyond sound
>   down(slowly
>   beneath
>   sight
> fall
>   ing(fall
>   ing through touch
>   less stillness(seized
> among what ghostly nevers of again)
> silent not night by silently unday
> life's bright less dwindled to a leastful most
> under imagination. When(out of sheer
>
> nothing)came a huger than fear a
>
> white with madness wind and broke oceans and tore
> mountains from their sockets and strewed the black air
> with writhing alive skies—and in death's place
> new fragrantly young earth space opening was.
> Were your eyes:lost,believing;hushed with when

Once again, a sonnet which, as you can see, is broken apart spatially in its first quatrain, but not arbitrarily, as you can also see, for the typography reinforces the "falling down" movement of the world drowning in rain. The opening negatives say that it was neither day nor night but somewhere eerily in between. Notice the repetition and variation of "silent unday etc." and "silent not night etc."

Then an enormous "white with madness wind" came and seemed to rip apart the landscape. But suddenly it was over, "and in death's place" was a fresh young earth opening up. The concluding line shifts without explanation or transition to the speaker's lover, as if watching the lover's eyes opening—as the earth opened—"lost,believing;hushed with when." Having been frightened out of their wits by this storm, they watch the skies open again, and they are stunned, as if having risen from the dead.

"When" is one of those adverbs of time Cummings likes to use as nouns, and it refers, whether indicatively or interrogatively, to some point in the future, whether near or far, at which time something will happen. The lover's eyes, then, are hushed with futurity, startled out of the immediate past of the storm, into the present of the ensuing calm, and quietly wondering what happens next. Clearly, they have died and been reborn, a transcendence *through* descendence. The way down is the way up.

5.

Our penultimate step toward acceptance includes those poems celebrating nature, children, individuals, and love, but without the need to intensify the positive by contrast with the negative. It's as if the object can now be celebrated on its own.

This poem is #XLVII in *1 x 1* (1944):

> until and i heard
> a certain a bird
> i dreamed i could sing
> but like nothing
>   are the joys
> of his voice
>
> until and who came
> with a song like a dream
> of a bird with a song
> like not anything
>   under skies
> over grass
>
> until and until
> into flame i can feel
> how the earth must fly
> if a truth is a cry
>   of a whole
> of a soul
>
> until i awoke
> for the beautiful sake
> of a grave gay brave
> bright cry of alive
>   with a trill

A poem which praises the song of this bird, it is very carefully built around a regular series of stanzas and of syntactical and spatial distortions well calculated not only to embody the speaker's reaction to the bird's song but also to suggest his answer, paradoxically countering the statement that his song is inferior to the *bird's*—by means of the very skill he shows in saying so. The joys of the bird's voice are "like nothing"—that is, "nothing like my song," and/or "like no other joys," and/or "like nothing in the phenomenal world—that is, noumenal, transcendent." The latter interpretation is further borne out by "song like a dream," "like not anything/under skies/over grass."

The rest of the poem carries through the suggestion that, until he can feel "how the earth must fly," he won't be able to sing as the bird sings, but the suggestion is also that he *will* be able to feel it, and that then he'll waken. This is a poem of pure celebration, the only contrasting element being the poet-speaker-singer himself, and he is absorbed, integrated, transformed, not only by means of the structure of the poem but also in the very act of praising itself.

6.

We reach, finally, that state of pure acceptance where, as Auden put it ("Lay your sleeping head, my love"), we find the mortal world enough—or, as we learn in Zen, where an act of complete attention reveals the true nature of things. We find in the following poem neither polarity nor transcendence of polarity, but rather a complete being-in-the-moment.

This is #3 from 95 *Poems* (1958), fittingly the last book of poems which Cummings saw through the press before his death four years later:

> now air is air and thing is thing:no bliss
>
> of heavenly earth beguiles our spirits,whose
> miraculously disenchanted eyes
>
> live the magnificent honesty of space.
>
> Mountains are mountains now;skies now are skies—
> and such a sharpening freedom lifts our blood
> as if whole supreme this complete doubtless

universe we'd(and we alone had)made

—yes;or as if our souls,awakened from
summer's green trance,would not adventure soon
a deeper magic:that white sleep wherein
all human curiosity we'll spend
(gladly,as lovers must)immortal and

the courage to receive time's mightiest dream

Another sonnet, this poem portrays lovers contemplating the autumn mid-point between summer and winter, and realizing that the "green trance" of summer is passing and the "white sleep" of winter has not yet arrived. Such a midpoint experience exposes them to the absolute and naked reality of the moment, without past or future, wherein the lovers paradoxically feel another kind of freedom—of being totally awake rather than in a state of trance or dream. "Mountains are mountains now;skies now are skies—," which echoes the Zen saying already mentioned above in chapter 2: Before one is enlightened, a mountain is only a mountain; when one learns *satori*, a mountain is a symbol of spirit; but after one experiences *satori*, a mountain is a mountain once again.

The point is, of course, that there is no *difference* between matter and spirit when the world is experienced in the moment, what Cummings called in his early essay on Gaston Lachaise, "the crisp organic squirm" of The Verb, The Is; or when he felt, while being imprisoned in France in 1917, that he could touch timelessness by abandoning the effort to keep track of time (*The Enormous Room*, beginning of chapter 5).

The paradox turns back on itself, however, when the speaker says that this sense of being wholly present makes us feel as if there will be no winter—that is, death—with its "deeper magic," as if "our souls . . . / would not adventure soon" into immortality or find "the courage to receive time's mightiest dream." Thus a conditional negative suggests, simply by being mentioned, its contrary—as when we say, "Try not to think of a white polar bear"—that in winter we'll reenter that *other* transcendent state of trance-dream-death, which in effect is precisely the same as the present state, that of being, as Cummings was fond of saying, supremely alive. One can truly die only if one has been actually alive; otherwise living, as he also would say, is merely "undying," while death is just "unliving."

7.

Transcendence, then, includes what we can dream as well as what we can experience when fully awake, for both are free of the polarities and categories of mundane perception. What is merely factual, as we have come to realize more fully since Kant and Blake, is not the same as what is wholly real or true—which is, as Wordsworth put it, both what we half perceive and half create. What we see is part of us, and we are a part of what we see. Reality arises from the interaction between the two; it is neither simply something "out there," nor is it merely imagined "in here"; what we see depends on *how* we see it; no measurement is free of the effect of the measuring instrument.

I read, in David Perkins' ambitious *History of Modern Poetry*, a disparagement of those who, like myself, see in Cummings something of a Zen master—as *he* puts it. But to read Cummings in terms of the conventional academic categories—whether old scholar, New Critic, or deconstructionist—is to miss the whole point. The study of oriental influences on Western literature has just begun to burgeon—a study upon which I myself have only recently embarked, but I hope I have pointed in the direction of that whole point.

As we read in the ancient Sanskrit of *The Upanishads*, "*Tat tvam asi*," what is out *there* is the same as what is in *here*. Brahman *is* Atman, the universal is *in* the particular, and there is no difference between the World Soul and our true nature within. That is the underlying theme, as Malcolm Cowley has pointed out,[3] in Whitman's "Song of Myself," and that is the tradition which the best of Cummings—and there is a *lot* of the best— follows.

part

two

:the

reception

6

E. E. Cummings and His Critics

We turn now to a consideration of how other critics have regarded
Cummings and of my responses to their views. The present chapter began
as a talk for a Modern Language Association panel on modern poetry chaired
by the late Hyatt H. Waggoner in December of 1962, and it represents an
attempt to sort out the history of Cummings criticism from 1922 to 1962.
Here I approach the problem of his relation to modernism from a somewhat different angle than that attempted in chapters 1 and 4 above. This
piece was subsequently published in *Criticism* in 1964.

I

I want in this essay to analyze the analyzers—the critics of Cummings—in
order to see what their views of the poet reveal about themselves, and what
this in turn reveals about the state of twentieth-century criticism and scholarship, its powers and limitations, during the heyday of the New Criticism.
Cummings is a very good test case, for, as we have seen, he is in the modernist tradition but not altogether of it: thus he has been attractive enough
to call forth much attention and approval, and yet he has been problematic
enough to cause much puzzlement and disapproval as well.

I do not want to be taken as saying, however, that those who dislike Cummings are always wrong and those who like him are always right. Certain of his admirers have just as incomplete a view of the case as certain of his attackers, and others of his attackers have set me to thinking very hard indeed. Hence I want to show what *I* think he is, and then to hold this up against what the *critics* think he is. And then I want to show how their judgments are governed by their interpretations, and how these in turn are governed by their critical preconceptions. I will suggest, finally, ways in which these preconceptions may be broadened.

II

Let us watch the critics now as they wrestle with the problem of interpreting and evaluating the writings of E. E. Cummings. I have read and analyzed roughly 325 essays and reviews concerning Cummings and his books, of varying length and quality, covering just forty years, and I want to report frankly that I was amazed and pleased to find that his supporters far outnumber his detractors: there are almost twice as many favorable items as in-between items, and almost three times as many in-betweens as unfavorable items (185:102:37).[1] But this doesn't leave me with nothing to do, for as I have already suggested, it is frequently the case that his admirers don't fully grasp the core of his work any more firmly than his detractors. I have divided the critics into decades, and we shall not be surprised to find that each decade views Cummings largely in the light of its own special preoccupations.

In the twenties, the decade in which Cummings published *The Enormous Room, Tulips and Chimneys, XLI Poems, is 5,* and *Him,* the main concern is technical: Cummings is viewed as a seeker after new forms for expressing the new sensibility of the age. Those who favor him praise his freshness, originality, and accuracy; he is viewed as a modern, but one with deep roots in the traditional, as one who can combine the ugly and the beautiful, gusto and tenderness; and his techniques are justified as necessary means to directness, precision, and immediacy. The in-betweens like his honesty, freshness, and lyricism, but disapprove of his concern with the ugly and with stylistic acrobatics. Those who disfavor him say the technical hijinks don't work and that they fail to conceal the real banality of what the poet is saying. But not much is said by anyone about the poet's vision of life, except that he is romantic, or modern, and this only superficially.

The thirties, which saw the publication *ViVa, Eimi, No Thanks, Tom,* and *Collected Poems,* emphasized the political. The lines are beginning to be drawn: Cummings is no longer seen as merely a poet of sensations rather than of thoughts, and the problem of individualism becomes central. He is defended as a romantic who protests against the prevailing system, and attacked correspondingly as an anti-rationalist and anarchist. The in-betweens regret the fact that a good poet is being spoiled by lack of growth in social vision. It is interesting to note how aesthetic and political matters tend to merge: for some, to see a poet standing for the living human being and his personal responses to life is an artistic as well as a social value, while for others, to see him retreating to the private vision is a violation of literary as well as of historical standards. What is not generally seen, however, is that the basis of Cummings' individualism does not fit into the political category at all, and that the whole issue is illusory to begin with.

In the forties, during which Cummings published *50 Poems, 1 x 1,* and *Santa Claus,* the fact that he does have a serious view of life is just being recognized, and the main issue is metaphysical. People like William Carlos Williams and Paul Rosenfeld are beginning to define the central transcendental vision, while other supporters are as usual content to praise his aliveness, freshness, immediacy, and so on. The related issue of the poet's growth is also receiving, naturally, more and more attention: Peter Munro Jack, Mizener, Blackmur, Arthos, R. P. Warren, and Trilling detect a developing maturity, while Bogan, Nemerov, Weiss, and Matthiessen find none. In-betweens and detractors are still doubting whether Cummings has any accessible vision at all, are wondering how far romantic sensationalism and anarchism can take a poet, and are complaining that Cummings offers no alternative to his rejection of the man-made world.

The fifties and the first few years of the sixties, the period which saw the publication of *Xaipe, i:SIX NONLECTURES, Poems: 1923–1954,* and *95 Poems,* focused on the moral issue of the poet's view of good and evil and of his attitude toward people. It is by now accepted that Cummings *does* have a view of life, but it is still not clear just what it is, especially whether or not it is complex and inclusive enough. In Haines, Maurer, Andrews, Wells, Logan, Watson, Wegner, and Mills can be found a growing recognition of Cummings' unifying and inclusive transcendentalism and mysticism, and this enables them to treat the poet as more than just a romantic individualist and to see him as steadily maturing. Beloof, Von Abele, and Graves also see growth in Cummings' art. The in-betweens like him but regret his refusal to grow and his simplistic view of the world. And the detractors see him as a solipsist who hates people and institutions, a poet lacking in the tragic sense and in the ability to respond to reality in all its complex fullness.

III

A fuller, more just and accurate view of the case will require some shifts in our critical perspective. The paradoxical vision of a transcendental world, which is at the center of Cummings' art and which explains its meaning, must be defined and placed in its historical context. This view, which achieves a vision of timelessness through time, is not a simplistic division of the universe into black and white: although it does divide the universe into the natural and artificial worlds, it is the latter which is, in his eyes, simplistic, while it is the organic world which reconciles opposites and resolves paradoxes—and this is, in effect, the complex and many-sided world which the critics say is lacking in his work.

Why don't they see it? Perhaps a few definitions and distinctions are in order. Modernism may be seen in terms of its three main influences: the metaphysical tradition, romanticism, and French symbolism. What has happened, however, is that modernism has been partial in its use of these influences, so that in some cases it has been forgotten how different modernism is, and in others how similar. In sum, modernism has tried to achieve romantic goals by metaphysical and symbolist means, and thus it has slighted metaphysical and symbolist goals as well as romantic methods. It has often been said that modernism is anti-romantic, but it is not often recognized that, in a certain sense, it is even more anti-metaphysical or anti-symbolist. Still less has it been realized that it is more pro-romantic than pro-metaphysical or pro-symbolist. If modernism combines metaphysical toughness, wit, and intelligence with symbolist evocativeness, ambiguity, and suggestiveness, where is the metaphysical sense of logical structure, where the symbolist sense of mystery? In fact, there is a certain way in which these two influences are contradictory, for the characteristic metaphysical pursuit of an argument produces quite a different sort of poem than that which results from the symbolist pursuit of the ineffable. Furthermore, if modernism has rejected romantic gush—the explicit, personal expression of emotion—where would it be without the romantic theory of organic form?

Such are the distinctions which we must work on—only suggested tentatively here—if we are to understand not only Cummings and romanticism, but also our own tradition as well. Although people such as Kermode, Langbaum, Bayley, Krieger, and Foster have already done the necessary spadework,[2] it is the failure of many other critics to make such distinctions which prevents them—friends and foes alike—from seeing what Cummings is actually saying. Scholars of romanticism and modernist critics must find ways of joining forces, for they have much to teach each other. The root cause of the modern lack of perceptiveness regarding romanticism, it seems to me, is that the moderns have taken over the romantic notion of organic form in art while retaining only a portion of the metaphysic from which it derives. That is why someone like the early Blackmur could complain of the absence of any known content in the poetry of E. E. Cummings. But the modernists agree with Coleridge and Cummings that, because the world is basically process rather than product, our approach to it must be exploratory and dynamic rather than fixed and static. That is why they want a poem to be ambiguous, ironic, and paradoxical: truth can only be glimpsed out of the corner of an eye. They also agree that, when it *is* glimpsed in those rare moments of unified vision, such moments represent transcendental intuitions of timelessness. But they believe that transcendence is achieved paradoxically by going down before one can go up, that unity is achieved by means of ambivalence, affirmation by negation. And they agree with Wordsworth that the world is what we half-create as well as what we perceive, that reality is a complex matter of the interplay between the external world and man's imaginative perception of it. But they disagree, in that the social world is for them one of the valid patterns which we both perceive and create. The modernists are concerned with Community and the Just Society; Cummings is not.

The modernists, when they reject Cummings' "simplistic" view, do not really mean that Cummings sees life as all joy and no sorrow—for time, death, failure, fear, and change are central to his vision, especially in the more recent work—but rather that Cummings rejects history, society, and their institutions. But to reject history, I may point out, is not to reject time but only its official version. Cummings does not say that institutions aren't *there*; he simply says, according to his organicist position, that because they are abstract they aren't real. But for the modernists, any writers worth their salt must reconcile their vision with the existence of institutions or run the risk of being called perpetual adolescents—as if that were the only alternative. And that is what modernism basically lacks: an appreciation that, if you don't believe in society, you *are* not necessarily a child; or, that if you are a child, maybe you are that best philosopher after all. Cummings, as well as Wordsworth, values the child not because it is cute and irresponsible and inexperienced, but rather because its perceptions are not yet bound by conventional categories. I would ask, with Sherwood Anderson, "isn't there at least a chance that the fear of emotional response to life may be as much a sign of immaturity as anything else?"[3]

Modernism lacks a consideration of alternatives; it is too monistic in its demand for a special kind of maturity, a peculiarly twentieth-century view of the tragic vision; and no amount of searching for "ceremony" and "tradition" will remedy this lack. Unless, of course, it is the oriental and romantic tradition of mystic and intuitive accord with natural process, a tradition in which suffering is not wished away but is rather accepted gladly as the condition of freedom. Ambiguity, I would suggest, is not the only way to achieve organic form in poetry, nor is ambivalence the only way to achieve transcendence.

7

Beyond Villains and Heroes?

This chapter was originally published in 1972 as the introduction to the collection of critical essays on Cummings which I edited for the Prentice-Hall Spectrum Twentieth Century Views series. It continues the effort, again from a somewhat different angle, to understand the critical response to Cummings and to suggest a way of reframing and enlarging that response.

I

As we have seen, Cummings' supporters have always outnumbered his detractors—and among the former he has had his share of very good critics indeed, critics who have been appreciative and discerning rather than merely adulatory, critics such as (and I name only the most conspicuous) Marianne Moore, Robert Graves, Ezra Pound, Allen Tate, and William Carlos Williams. And among those who, while they may not be counted among his supporters, nevertheless have seen fit to take him seriously are found Edmund Wilson, Kenneth Burke, Louis MacNeice, Robert Penn Warren, and John Crowe Ransom.

Yet, in spite of such criticism and a continuing and flourishing popularity in many circles, there exists about his reputation an aura of inadequacy, a sense of some important establishment to which he has failed to gain admission, an air of unseriousness about his stature, as if he were somehow good but not quite good enough. Not that I think this anomalous position bothered Cummings, or that we need to find some means of sanctioning his career for the academy—did he not relish his position as an individualist, a nonconformist, one who would go his own way no matter what?

It is about ourselves that I am concerned and the deprivation we inflict upon our lives by mistaken exclusions. I am concerned about our understanding of our poetic heritage, about the powers and limitations of our critical fashions, and about the reading lists, anthologies, and matters of instruction in our schools, colleges, and universities. I want to ask what it is that has caused us to attribute to Cummings that slight flavor of illegitimacy, and I want to suggest how it may be remedied. For I think we are ready now for a fairer assessment of the case.

II

In the 1920s Cummings was known as a conspicuous member of the avant-garde, an arch-experimentalist, a modernist, and a bohemian. The New Criticism, which was just beginning to germinate in the writings of T. E. Hulme, Ezra Pound, T. S. Eliot, and I. A. Richards, had not yet noticed any serious discrepancy between its own principles and the writings of Cummings. Whatever hostility he aroused was among the antimodernists—Max Eastman and Stanton A. Coblentz, for example, and, in later decades, critics such as John Sparrow and Ivor Winters—men who were attacking Pound and Eliot as well. There is no real problem here, for while it cannot be said that the critics, favorable or otherwise, really understood what Cummings was about, neither can it be said that he himself had altogether found his way. It was suspected—and it was probably partly the case at the time—that he was a poet of sensations rather than of thoughts, and this notion has continued to haunt his reputation ever since, despite the obvious fact that he did in fact develop a vision of life as he matured. Indeed, it is one of the great flaws of Cummings criticism that it has pretty consistently failed to develop as *he* developed, that it has remained fixated upon early attitudes to his early work.

In the 1930s firmer lines began to be drawn. It was becoming clear by then that Cummings was antirational, anticollectivist, and antipolitical, both in theme and technique, and that he was therefore a threat to another kind of antimodernist—the leftist critic. To be sure, many regarded these qualities favorably, seeing in a poet who stood for the living human being and his personal responses to life a social as well as an artistic value. Yet even the emerging New Criticism, spearheaded in this case by the austere R. P. Blackmur, although pleased with Cummings' concern for experimentation and his dislike of mass culture, was made uneasy by his romantic vagueness and his ostensibly simplistic answers to the times. The affirmation of love, spring, and the individual did not seem a sufficiently serious reaction to the tragedy of twentieth-century history, which was then reaching its climax in a depression and in preparations for a second world war.

In the 1940s critics such as Paul Rosenfeld, William Carlos Williams, Theodore Spencer, and Lloyd Frankenberg realized that there was more to Cummings than this, that underlying his interest in love, spring, and the individual was a vision that served to give depth and meaning to both his anarchic techniques and his anarchistic beliefs. In describing this vision, however, they were still more or less limited to such concepts as freshness, originality, accuracy, directness, precision, and immediacy, and they therefore produced no full and consistent analysis of the character of his thought. Hostile critics such as F. O. Matthiessen and Robert Martin Adams could, therefore, still dismiss him as an adolescent sentimentalist and sensationalist despite the fact that he had vividly recorded at first hand two of the most significant events of our century—the beginnings in World War I of concentration-camp existence, and the subsequent rise of the Soviet state.

The demand on Cummings to develop—to be more "mature," more sophisticated, more aware of how good and evil are intermingled, and more appreciative of the meaning of history and society—increased during the 1950s. Though it was still not realized that an appreciation of his qualities required terms and concepts that had not yet been evolved, several critics—George Haines IV, Robert E. Maurer, John Logan, Barbara Watson, and Ralph J. Mills, Jr.—were already pushing beyond the customary notions of freshness and precision, moving deeper toward concepts of transcendence, mysticism, and timelessness, and S. V. Baum and Rudolph Von Abele were conducting detailed analyses of techniques and themes. Unfortunately the New Criticism's methods of close analysis, which had by now become fairly standard in college and university courses in literature and criticism, did not often suit Cummings' poems very well, for the kinds of irony, paradox, ambivalence, ambiguity, and symbolism favored by that method were frequently not to be found there.

* * *

Nevertheless, as the fifties gave way to the sixties and seventies, a sharper awareness of the nature of his vision gradually emerged. It became clear, for one thing, that we were significantly hampered by the limits of contemporary criticism, since he wrote to a large degree outside of these limits. Eliot and Stevens and Auden, for example, were easier to deal with critically, for they wrote within them. Even when we know we *like* Cummings, we lack the appropriate language for explaining why. Theoretically, our problem is to expand our ideas of what constitutes valid poetry; practically, it is to find out what other kinds of poets we think are worthwhile—apart from and in addition to those who have the "unified sensibility" that the New Critics have taught us to appreciate. We must, in other words, widen our historical and critical frames of reference.

III

Take the matter of love, for instance. Although Cummings is no mere "romantic" love poet and has written some of the most direct poems about sex in the language, the fact remains that he does not always depict the worm within the rose, the skull beneath the skin. His characteristic love poems are based on a single wholeness of feeling—praise, reverence, joy, passion, devotion—rather than upon the mixed feelings favored by the New Criticism. He is perfectly aware that his lady is mortal, that she sweats, and that she performs the natural functions, but he prefers to go beyond that awareness toward moments of affirmation. If we compare his "somewhere i have never travelled,gladly beyond" (*ViVa*, # LVII) to Auden's "Lay your sleeping head, my love," for example, we find that Cummings' emotion is not "qualified"—but that does not mean that it is sentimental. His singleness comes not from simplifying, but rather from transcendence, which is a different thing altogether.

When it comes to the means by which such an emotion is embodied— structure, technique, style—Cummings is indeed an innovator and, as such, is in line with the predispositions of contemporary critics. Although he is more traditional than he often seems at first glance, he was never content to rest easily within inherited conventions. Here again, instead of favoring the more usual devices of the modernists—juxtaposition, self-mockery, reflexive meanings, complex symbols, learned allusions—Cummings went on to develop a number of his own. Thus he juxtaposes words and parts of words instead of images, anecdotes, and incidents, and his chief structural invention is typographical—or perhaps linguistic—rather than semantic. He distorts grammar and syntax by changing word order and parts of speech instead of exploiting the many levels of meaning in the connotations of words.

He aims at simultaneity and instantaneousness, then, rather than at irony and ambiguity; at reawakening encapsulated meanings rather than at multiplying them. He often writes lyrics that are truly lyrical—poems that are, in the best sense, like songs—for he aims at joyfulness rather than at meditativeness, and the result is more musical and melodious, while at the same time authentic, than any love poetry since the sixteenth and seventeenth centuries.

On the other side, of course, there is hate. It would be hard to find satires as barbed and brilliant as his after the eighteenth century, for if there is venom—and we have tried to place that in perspective in chapter 5—there is exuberance and joy too in Cummings' hate, and a good number of his satires are spirited, witty, and large-hearted. As for the rest, satire is no more a typical modernist genre than is the love lyric, both of which require more single-mindedness than the New Criticism allows. If contemporary critics agree with Cummings' attacks on a mechanized civilization, they do not agree with the basis of that attack or with the implied or expressed solution, for it is not so much the individual they would rescue as society.

The characteristic modernist genre is, in fact, either the meditative lyric or the meditative archetypal-mythic "epic" (or some combination of the two), and Cummings has written neither. He is not, however, a simple one- or two-note man. In addition to the love lyric and the satire, he works typically, as we have seen, with the descriptive and reflective nature poem—which, significantly, deals as often with urban as with rural landscapes—and with poems about, and in praise of, people.

It is a matter of expectations, then, and the criticism of the first half of this century formed a set of expectations that Cummings often did not meet—expectations about feeling, about techniques, and about genres. So too it was with the expectation about artistic growth and development. Yeats set the pattern, making himself over three times during a long and fruitful career. Pound put behind him the lyrics of his earlier period to go on to *The Cantos*—as Hart Crane and William Carlos Williams went on to their "epics." Eliot progressed from "Prufrock" to *The Waste Land*, through *Ash Wednesday* to the *Four Quartets*, and on to the later plays. Auden went from

Marx to Freud to Christianity. Cummings simply became more Cummings, and so the impression has gained currency that he has not changed, not matured. There are different kinds of growth, however, and one can develop and deepen along a single course as well as reverse oneself or take up a new tack; one way is not necessarily more mature than the other. Stevens, although more sophisticated and ambivalent than Cummings, developed pretty much along the lines he had laid down early in his career. So did Frost, as another example, and Marianne Moore.

The fact is that Cummings changed quite markedly all through his life. His love poetry, for example, became less erotic and more transcendental. His typography exploded—and then imploded. His linguistic distortions became more meaningful and luminous. Most important of all, his vision of life deepened and crystallized to a degree not sufficiently appreciated by the critics, for their expectations about vision were the most limiting of all.

IV

The world in which the New Criticism conceived of itself and its favored authors as living is the world that has been created by History up to now. It is a world that has become more and more fragmented since the seventeenth century—or the Middle Ages, or perhaps even the Serpent in Eden—and which artists and cultivated people must try to put back together before it is too late.

But there is another version of the world—equally archetypal, equally religious—that says that the hope of redemption is now, that nature and human life have but to be seen freshly in order to be experienced freshly. History is the result of mental rigidity, a nightmare from which we can awaken. The way to improvement is not by finding the right set of discriminations, but rather by denying the principle of discrimination itself. Such a world will not lack values; rather they will emerge and fade, grow and die, in a natural way. Thus a revolution in consciousness can bring about a revolution of the world.

The ultimate awareness we must try to grasp, according to this second world view, as I have been attempting to show, is not so much an *integration* of polarities—thought and feeling, for example—as a rising *above* them. It is the result of an attempt not to control and understand the world, but rather to accept and experience it. It says that timelessness is attained when past and future become less important than absorption in the present moment—where a sense of the eternal Now can permeate consciousness. It is an achievement beyond the will to achieve, a transcendence of categories, a strength strong enough to surrender and forgive—surrender our need to control, forgive the world for not living up to our expectations. Taoist wisdom, with which Cummings was familiar, puts it this way:

> The man in whom Tao
> Acts without impediment
> . . . is not always looking
> For right and wrong
> Always deciding "Yes" or "No."[1]

And so Cummings says, at the conclusion of his introduction to *Collected Poems* (1938): "Never the murdered finalities of wherewhen and yesno,impotent nongames of wrongright and rightwrong;never to gain or pause,never the soft adventure of undoom,greedy anguishes and cringing ecstasies of inexistence;never to rest and never to have:only to grow."

This attitude underlies Cummings' work from the beginning. It shows up specifically in his first volumes of the early 1920s in such poems as "o sweet spontaneous" (*Tulips & Chimneys*, 58), and in 1926 in such well-known pieces as "voices to voices,lip to lip" (*is 5*, ONE, #XXXIII), and "since feeling is first" (*is 5*, FOUR, #VII). It grows deeper and steadier throughout his career, appearing as a contrast to the societal world in his satires; as a basis for love poems; as emerging from some intense moment of responsiveness to a vivid experience of the natural world; as a basis for praising individuals and lovers; and as a way of talking about harmony with and surrender to natural process over and above the usual polarities. Compare, for example, "one's not half two. It's two are halves of one" (*1 x 1*, #XVI); the familiar "what if a much of a which of a wind" (*1 x 1*, #XX); and "dive for dreams" (*95 Poems*, #60), which concludes:

> never mind a world
> with its villains or heroes
> (for god likes girls
> and tomorrow and the earth)

V

Let us now take a single poem and look at it more closely in order to give weight to my central point and to illustrate its usefulness:

> being to timelessness as it's to time,
> love did no more begin than love will end:
> where nothing is to breathe to stroll to swim
> love is the air the ocean and the land
>
> (do lovers suffer?all divinities
> proudly descending put on deathful flesh:
> are lovers glad?only their smallest joy's
> a universe emerging from a wish)
>
> love is the voice under all silences,
> the hope which has no opposite in fear;
> the strength so strong mere force is feebleness:
> the truth more first than sun more last than star
>
> —do lovers love?why then to heaven with hell.
> Whatever sages say and fools,all's well
>   (95 *Poems*, #94)

This is one of the many poems in which Cummings praises love and lovers, and as such it is in the great tradition of the love lyric from Catullus to the courtly troubadours and from the Elizabethans to the romantics—as we see, the poem is a sonnet—in treating erotic love in an exalted way. So much is clear from a first and second reading, and so much has been fully acknowledged by the critics. After seeing these things we can say either that the poem is fine, if a bit archaic, or that it is, for these times, downright silly and sentimental. But then, if we continue to allow the poem to speak to us, we begin to notice that the diction, syntax, rhythm, ideas, imagery, structure, and so on, reflect Cummings' special consciousness and style. The opening word, for example, by virtue of its place in the line, does double duty as a verb and as a noun—meaning "since love is" and also implying "state of existence." Further, the first line as a whole is based on Cummings' characteristic use of what Lloyd Frankenberg calls "the algebra of the heart"[2]—since x is to y as x is to z. As we shall see, the meaning of "nothing" in the third line is both ordinary and Cummingsesque, and the concept of lovers as divinities is both conventional and special. The poem exemplifies neither mere traditional hyperbole nor modernist ambivalence. It is, rather, a way of seeing love in terms of the alternative world view.

Since love stands in the same relation to timelessness as it does to time—that is, having no reference either to time or to its opposite and thereby standing outside of the whole polarity—it does not exist in the world of History. In that other world where "nothing" exists—that is, that world above the world of ordinary perceptions and habits—love is the "something," the substance—put, it may be noticed, in terms of nature, for the natural world is the ground of that reality grasped by the vision of transcendence.

So far, then, love has been taken out of the usual categories and placed in the world without categories—or rather, it has been identified with its "material." The second stanza begins by putting this "definition" in an explicitly religious context: lovers are seen as sacrificial gods who put on mortality for the sake of redeeming mankind. The point is that those who possess such an awareness must perforce enact their destiny in the ordinary world, and this is a form of suffering (compare Cummings' "Foreword to Krazy"). On the other hand, the joy of lovers creates worlds out of wishes—which might seem sentimental if it were not for the counterposing context of their pain. Their wishes create worlds not because love is simply a fantasy of fulfillment, but rather because the inner reality reflects the outer.

After love has been placed in the world without categories and then defined in relation to the ordinary world, its nature must be exemplified in terms of this ordinary world, for it is difficult to understand things in any other terms. This Cummings does by playing on the usual polarities of sound and silence, hope and fear, strength and weakness, day and night, and then canceling them out. He takes extremes and puts love beyond them: it is the sound within silence, the strength beyond force, a truth that extends from before daybreak until after nightfall (echoing and developing "love did no more begin than love will end").

Finally, when lovers love, hell becomes a part of heaven—thereby abolishing *that* fatal polarity—and whatever either sages or fools say, all is well. It does not matter whether wise men or stupid men say anything, for love is beyond wisdom and stupidity and has nothing to do with how we may intellectualize or verbalize about it. Thus are opposites transcended.

The reason, therefore, that Cummings does not display the self-mockery, ambivalence, struggle before affirmation, and other characteristics prized by modern criticism, as I have been arguing, is that his vision is directed toward a state of unified awareness beyond, outside of, and apart from such conflicts. This is not to say that it is easy, for it is a rare and difficult thing and not to be confused with promiscuous self-abandonment. Giving up the principle of categories, surrendering to a reality experienced directly, daring to act out one's deepest and innermost being: these attainments are not to be confused with what many do who think of themselves as spontaneous and original when they are only skimming the top off themselves and evading rather than facing the actual job of self-realization and self-transcendence.

VI

Thus it is possible to define a kind of poetry that is valid although it falls outside the critically fashionable definitions—a kind of poetry that Cummings wrote for forty years. Poems written in this mode do not need to find the villain within, for theirs is a world beyond villains and heroes.

Or it should be. And here we confront a dilemma, for the world of Cummings' poems does have, as we have seen, its villains and heroes, and they crop up not only in the satires but also in the love lyrics. If a good lover is also a good hater, his hate will be tempered by forgiveness. It is easy to explain the *presence* of villains in the satires; it is less easy to account for the quality and intensity of some of Cummings' *feelings* about them—scorn, for example, or contempt, or condescension—as if Cummings were indeed blaming the world for not living up to his expectations.

☆   ☆   ☆

In Cummings' own terms, while it might be appropriate to reject the non- and anti-transcendental, it is not appropriate to despise it.[3] A man who has gone beyond ambivalence is obliged by his own attainment, as I have already suggested, to feel sympathy for those who have not yet made it. A man who is at peace with himself may not suffer fools gladly, and he may energetically work toward correcting the abuses of society, but he should not betray that self-congratulatory reaction, concealing a lack of self-confidence, that is sometimes found in Cummings. For his own teachings amount to a rejection not only of stereotypes and categories but also of spite. When Krazy Kat is hit by a brick, a heart flowers in the "balloon" above her head; when Cummings was hit by a brick, too often he replied with savage invective. In consequence, he sometimes projects a feeling of us-against-them that offends many and that gainsays his own view of life. Even in a love lyric he will sometimes pause to negate something or somebody, thereby betraying, through overinsistence, a certain defensiveness:

> and here is a secret they never will share
> for whom create is less than have . . .
> that we are in love,that we are in love:
> with us they're nothing times nothing to do . . .
>
> this world(as timorous itsters all
> to call their cowardice quite agree)
> shall never discover our touch and feel. . . .
>> (*Xaipe*, #66)

Is his love the more valuable in proportion to the few who can share it?

I do not agree that poetry always needs the tension of opposites, but I would agree that if you *do* polarize, you should not violate your audience's sense of reality by cleanly dividing the world into villains and heroes. You cannot apply the mood of certainty, which is appropriate to the transcendent world, to the social criticism of this world, where it is not appropriate. The appropriate mood of one who transcends, when he turns from the ecstasy of his vision to contemplate the ordinary world—as Cummings himself has shown us—is surrender, love, and forgiveness. As he wrote in the legend attached to Mrs. Cummings' photograph of Marianne Moore in *Adventures in Value* ([1962] IV 3):

> in a cruel world—to show mercy. . . .
> in a hateful world—to forgive

Or, to quote again from Chuang Tzu:

> [The Taoist man]
> Does not bother with his own interests
> And does not despise others who do. . . .
> He goes his way
> Without relying on others
> And does not pride himself
> On walking alone.
> While he does not follow the crowd
> He won't complain of those who do. . . .[4]

Either this, or you must be ambivalent—you must see that what you hate in others is also in yourself. If you do not transcend the categories, then you must play the category game wisely and humanely. Complacency, spite, and defensiveness are a false combination as well as an unattractive one. Thus, though I cannot agree with the cavils of some of Cummings' critics, I do agree that a lack of charity is troubling. Cummings was not always strong enough himself to surrender, love, and forgive, and one needs an especial strength to surrender, love, and forgive oneself.

Cummings was shy, sensitive, and self-protective in the extreme: it must have been very difficult for him to strive toward the givingness and openness he sang of so often and so well—as indeed it is difficult for any of us. It is a sign of the magnitude of his achievement that he got as far as he did; even the question I have been discussing, if I am right, is best viewed as evidence of the intensity of the struggle as well as of the preciousness of the attainment. None of his contemporaries is without his own blind spot. Pound, Eliot, Frost, Stevens, and even Yeats are all shortsighted, cranky, and eccentric in certain ways.

What then has Cummings left us? On the simplest and most basic level, he has significantly expanded the language, not so that we may imitate his tricks and devices, but rather that we may develop a greater sense of its possibilities for ourselves. Few poets have done more with words than he; his sense of and delight in style were extraordinarily vivid, musical, and almost tactile. Further, he carried on and developed, as we have seen, the tradition of the lyric, of lyric style and structure, to an extent which has not been surpassed in our time even by Yeats. In his satires, whatever their occasional failings, he was among the first in our time to point out and diagnose the most dangerous features of our society—features which, alas, seem to have gotten worse as he wrote, and which have been provoking more and more desperate reactions among us ever since. Finally, when he reaches those moments of pure transcendence—as he does often—he gives us something more important than any merely clairvoyant social criticism. He gives us a vision of what it means to achieve, beyond achievement, our full and fully human potential:

> (now the ears of my ears awake and
> now the eyes of my eyes are opened)
>   (*Xaipe*, #65)

8

"Epiphanies Are Hard to Come By"

:Cummings' Uneasy Mask and the Divided Audience

This piece was written for the 1983 *Resources for American Literary Study* as an essay-review of Lloyd Dendinger's 1981 collection of reviews of Cummings' publications, *E. E. Cummings: The Critical Reception.* Thus, it represents another way of assessing the development of Cummings criticism.

I

This book continues the production of scholarly aids to the study of Cummings—which includes Firmage's bibliography and his edition of Cummings' essays, Dupee and Stade's edition of Cummings' letters, Rotella's bibliography of secondary criticism, and Kennedy's biography—and as such is a welcome addition, enabling us, as these other contributions do, to place the published *oeuvre* in a broader and deeper perspective. The present volume gives a full sampling of the reviews of Cummings' books in the order of publication, shows "what his contemporaries thought of him," and contributes to that chapter of literary history covered by the poet's life.

Here we have a representative collection of reviews of Cummings' books during his lifetime—from *The Enormous Room* in 1922 to *95 Poems* in 1958. As Dendinger explains, "Most of the newspaper reviews are to be found in the Cummings collection at Harvard University's Houghton Memorial Library. These reviews are in eight scrapbooks kept principally by Cummings' mother, dating from as early as 1912." I remember these scrapbooks well, for the Cummingses were kind enough to lend them to me many years ago when I began to prepare my first book-length study of the poet. I made and have kept a card file of their contents, and I have made use of this file in various ways. But time, alas, has not been kind to the original scrapbooks. "They are in terrible condition," Dendinger continues. "The scrapbooks themselves, to say nothing of the clippings, are disintegrating with age. Each time I returned one from the Houghton reading room, it left its outline on the reading table in the powdered dust of its own substance."

At the very least, then, he has rescued them yet awhile from oblivion. Certainly, many of them—by anonymous and unknown reviewers, and in out-of-the-way papers—could have been allowed to slip silently to their fate, except for the fact that they *do* help us to understand the poet by allowing us to know "what his contemporaries," and not just his expert and knowledgeable contemporaries, "thought of him," and especially by allowing us to understand the very crucial role of modernism in our literary history between the two wars.

II

Dendinger's own introduction provides some useful guidelines. The most frequent and pressing problems raised by these reviews, he indicates, are Cummings' unique way with language, his experimental typography, and the puzzling relationship between his modernism of form and traditionalism of subject. Dendinger makes the telling point that Pound and Eliot also present traditional subjects in experimental forms, and that it was Williams and Stevens who sought "to make the subject as well as the form of poetry new." They nevertheless all share a common concern "to revitalize poetry and, through poetry, language." Then, in line with Laura Riding and Robert Graves' much earlier demonstration in their 1927 *Survey of Modernist Poetry*, he argues that, if you take away Cummings' "tricks," you take away the poetry. "Form has become subject," as with the other modernists.

The issue of modernism is crucial in trying to come to terms both with this almost forty-year collection of reviews and, as I have shown, with Cummings himself. These reviews can be usefully treated in terms of two major chronological groups, each culminating and shifting, naturally enough, around the publication of his "collected poems," the first in 1938, and the second in 1954. Although Dendinger notes some shifts occurring around these dates, he still concludes that "the principal themes of the commentary were established fairly early and the reviewers of the latter two decades largely concerned themselves with topics defined in the first two." This may be true, as far as "themes" and "topics" are concerned, but there is somewhat more to be said about the difference between earlier and later reviewers in how they *handle* them.

By and large, the reviewers of the first nine volumes, 1922–1935, are fairly evenly split—although both groups see him as modernist—between those who favor him for his modernism and those who don't. What is on trial is not so much Cummings as modernism itself, a nascent and revolutionary modernism which is just beginning to make its way into the American popular press. Thus Cummings is frequently compared to Stein, Joyce, Pound, Eliot, and the like. (The year 1922, the date of *The Enormous Room*, of course, also saw the appearance of *Ulysses* and *The Waste Land*). It is difficult for us today, after Cummings' modernism has come to be seriously questioned, as we have seen, to appreciate how much clearer the issue seemed then: Cummings was deemed to be, for better or worse, among the foremost of the avant-garde and experimental writers and artists. Of course, to a degree, he *was* more experimental (and less developed in vision) in those days than he subsequently became, so it is only natural for him to have been lumped together with the other modernists.

Nevertheless, what we witness here is the consternation of many anonymous and unknown reviewers, in out-of-the-way papers, confronted by what they don't understand and can't come to terms with. The literary historian might be reminded of the similar baffled reception that certain romantics and pre-Raphaelites received in the previous century. And even at the hands of—as also with Cummings—some then-distinguished literary persons. As one anonymous—but expert and knowledgeable—reviewer in *Variety* in 1933 put it, "Guys like E. E. Cummings are unfair. They write important books in such a manner as to give unimportant 'critics' a chance to puff up and parade their ignorance." Their reaction to the unfamiliar is not simply defensive; it is, rather, rejecting. As is still the case today—it can happen to any of us—when we are faced with strange and peculiar art forms.

So we read the first words in this book, a review of *The Enormous Room* by Robert Littell in *New Republic*: "I feel as if I had been rooting long, desperate hours in a junk heap." Yet he still manages to emerge admiring the book, a testimony to his underlying critical toughness. Less hardy is William Russell Clark on *XLI Poems* in the *Galveston News*, who calls Cummings "the young Lochinvar of unintelligibility." Or, even more proud of his provincial attitude is J. G. N., reviewing *is* 5 with heavy sarcasm in the *Kansas City Journal-Post:* "Highly sophisticated critics, actually living in New York, have advised us [that Cummings is a great poet]—and there are some 10,000,000 people in New York! It is possibly true, as some irreverent person may object, that the 10,000,000 are largely kikes; but size is much, and New York is very big. Etc."

But an undertone of admiration manages to lurk beneath the surface of even some of these negative reviews, and Cummings is seen as a poet with "genuine lyric gifts," though he perversely insists upon burying them beneath these annoying modernist gimmicks—a theme to which we will return in due course. In the meantime, "highly sophisticated critics" such as John Dos Passos, John Peale Bishop, Marianne Moore, Malcolm Cowley, S. Foster Damon, Paul Rosenfeld, and so on, are aware that something crucial has been going on in Western culture since the nineteenth century, and especially since the First World War, that this has affected the forms of art, and that Cummings is among the chief representatives of this movement.

⁂ ⁂ ⁂

Says Dos Passos admiringly of *The Enormous Room*, in the *Dial*, "This sort of thing knocks literature into a cocked hat," echoing Verlaine's "take eloquence and wring its neck." Bishop writes of the same book in *Vanity Fair*, "I doubt if any other could have informed physical squalor, beastliness and degradation with so splendid a spiritual irradiance." Cowley explains, in analyzing the poet's techniques (in *ViVa*) in *New Republic*, that the issue is "how, after three thousand years of written literature, to say anything new, or anything old in a new way."

The problem for readers, then as now, with the modernist movement—which I take to have begun around the end of the nineteenth century and which I believe continues in various forms today—is basically this: to be able to deal with the fragmented, the disagreeable, the difficult, the painful, and the threatening, and to be able to feel that there is somehow something to be gained by so dealing. This is not simply an aesthetic or cultural problem—it is also a psychological, if not a spiritual, one. In speaking of the "untranslatability" of modern poetry, Dendinger rightly says, "This is, of course, true of all poetry, but it is a matter of degree and much more important in those periods where formal considerations take precedence over everything else. And the definitive formal characteristic of the modern period is fragmentation."

What we are facing—and have been facing since the late eighteenth century—is the challenge, on the one hand, that we can become more human than ever before in history, and the threat, on the other, that we are becoming more dehumanized. As a result, our very relationship to reality—the reality of ourselves, of society, and of the earth—is in danger. If we are to heal this split, we must be able to confront, to begin with, the fragmented, the disagreeable, the difficult, the painful, and the threatening in *ourselves*. This is the underlying spirit of modernist art, and those who believe we can live comfortably and sanely without such questioning, and who can merely see a negative end to the negative way, rather than spiritual irradiance, can only reject it. Those who see, on the contrary, along with Cummings, that "to create is first of all to destroy" (quoted from *The Enormous Room* by Gilbert Seldes in his *Double Dealer* review), who feel that the way down is the way up, can only welcome it.

The issue, then, for the first dozen years or so—although a few modernist critics themselves, such as Edmund Wilson, R. P. Blackmur, Conrad Aiken, William Carlos Williams, William Troy, and Kenneth Burke are not always wholly favorable—is not so much Cummings as it is modernism itself. With the appearance of *Collected Poems* in 1938, however, the time for serious assessment of the poet had arrived, and the lines among the modernist critics themselves were beginning to be drawn. In other words, since modernism had by then had a chance to establish itself, not only among writers and artists but also in the minds of critics and reviewers, the question became one of whether and how much Cummings was, in fact, a representative figure of that movement. And naturally this leads to questions of what the exact meaning of that movement is in the first place.

III

Dudley Fitts, writing in the *Saturday Review of Literature*, says, "It was time for this book. Cummings has had more than his share of irrelevant criticism, whether adulatory or scornful. Everyone will talk about him, classify him, define him; few seem to have read him with critical attention." Doing precisely that, Paul Rosenfeld points out in the *Nation* the two characteristics of Cummings' poetry which "solidly set it in the category of the modern." The first is his "similarity to the fauve and cubist painters and sculptors" in his dislocations of language and typography; the second is his blending of the metaphysical and romantic traditions in his unique combination of wit and musicality. S. I. Hayakawa writes in *Poetry* of Cummings' descent from the paradise of childhood into the hell of the modern city and modern warfare, and suggests that this fact may explain the eccentricities of his technique—as partly a disguise and partly an attempt to achieve accuracy and immediacy of presentation. Morton Dauwen Zabel claims similarly in the *Southern Review* that they "are integral to the whole intensity and anguish of his senses in the face of 'the essential horror' he has confronted."

Rolfe Humphries, on the other hand, in the *New Masses*, while granting him "tenderness, a fair ear (about as subtle, for example, as Swinburne's), imagination, invention, and wit," at the same time asserts that "what he lacked was control, balance." Furthermore, Humphries says, his anarchistic vision is self-defeating: "Where the idea is that nothing triumphant can be good, it surely follows that nothing good can be triumphant." W. T. S. (whom I take to be Winfield Townley Scott) in the *Providence Journal* has it that "the sad thing about him is that his work has become progressively more hysterical and less vital." And Horace Gregory in the *New Republic* brings up a charge which is destined to echo down the halls of Cummings' reputation for many a year to come: Cummings has "become the Jazz Age Peter Pan," "fixed in rigid attitudes of youth," because of his continuing defiance of the ruling powers and values of the modern world. Gregory continues: "In this defiance, there is less snobbery than evidence of fear: fear of being misunderstood, fear of being less than unique, fear of the many rising against the few and, over all, a complex and contradictory fear of loneliness." "Part of Mr. Cummings' difficulty in finding an immediate audience," he adds, "may be traced to the uneasy mask he wears."

Such contrast between praise and blame among respectable and informed critics may seem to argue for absolute relativism in criticism and make committed deconstructionists of us all. I would suggest, however, that if we acknowledge valid reason on both sides, we might come a bit closer to the whole truth about Cummings. For one thing, while some cogency may be granted to such views as Gregory's, for example, the negative critics tend to miss the artistic *complexity* of Cummings which the positive ones see, the *context* and the *rationale* of the poet's vision and techniques. If we take the anarchism, the youthfulness, and the hysteria and place them in relation to fauvism and cubism, the metaphysical and romantic traditions, the descent into hell, and the need for immediacy of effect, we will be able to see these supposed deficiencies in a somewhat more intelligible framework. That is to say, in response to a certain kind of experience, in terms of certain artistic traditions, and by means of a certain kind of sensibility, Cummings is trying to achieve a certain kind of new combination of elements: "unable to go further with either the sheerly witty or the lyrical, romantic type of poet," as Rosenfeld explains, Cummings is "making a third, possibly twentieth-century sort by joining the elements of the other two."

Why, then, do some supposedly modernist critics fail to see this? The other thing is that the answer must be found partly in something about Cummings himself, some weakness not specified by them but which is nevertheless implied by Gregory: Cummings fails of reasonable success in *convincing* potentially sympathetic and knowledgeable readers of the true context and rationale of his art. Somewhere deep within, he is at odds with himself—and with his audience. What I think this inner conflict means, as I have already suggested and will show in greater detail below in chapters 10 and 12, is reflected in his characteristic attempt to appear joyous and confident, thereby depriving his art and his readers of the true context of inner struggle which gives significance to his vision and techniques.

As for the problem with his audience, the symptoms are clear, as Gregory indicates, in the introduction to these *Collected Poems.* If the problem with "mostpeople," as we have seen, is that they cannot accept the way down as the way up, the trouble with Cummings is that he cannot accept *them.* And yet the other clear message in this introduction, which I take to be his "real" message, is one of openness, acceptance, abolition of categories, and devotion to the living processes of organismic being. The result is an "uneasy mask": a split in vision leads to a failure of rhetoric, for he does not allow for the possibility that his poems could change the unconvinced— who, of course, have no choice, really, but to reciprocate by remaining outside the charmed circle drawn for them. His deepest fear must have been not simply of being misunderstood but rather of his *own* difficulty, illustrated precisely in the opening words of this introduction, in being open and accepting, which he therefore projected onto "mostpeople." This is a projection which polarizes unduly some of his lyrics of joy and many of his satires, as shown above in chapter 5, and thereby deprives them of much of their power to engage the unconvinced. Otherwise, he would not have had always to appear joyous and confident and consequently to surround himself with so many boundaries. The "contradictions" of Emerson and Whitman are in the spirit of inclusiveness; those of Cummings run counter to that spirit.

The issue may be brought into clearer focus if we look closely at the two key reviews in this section. The *Partisan Review* published a negative piece by Philip Horton, balanced it with a positive one by Sherry Mangan, and entitled the pair, in a nonpartisan spirit, "Two Views of Cummings." Horton begins by claiming that nothing has changed in Cummings over a period of fifteen years and that "the notorious typography" is a "historical curiosity." Nor does he approve of the "sexires" or the satires and says that the mingling of the trivial and the serious, the confusion of values, result from "his deliberate rejection of knowledge." He notes that the introduction, while it appears to embrace and affirm, in fact "reduces to negation and rejection." The rejection of knowledge can only lead to "the scattered impulses of an immature personality." Horton's polarization itself commits the either/or fallacy in denying the role of emotions and the body in regulating the personality, and it sounds perilously close to the merely conventional dispraise of Cummings, until we recall that Horton is the biographer of Hart Crane—and also that it is one of the less tenable doctrines of the New Critical version of modernism that the artist must "develop" and "mature" in certain stated ways, a doctrine already reflected in Gregory's review. Yet we cannot easily dismiss what Horton says about the introduction.

Mangan, to her credit, puts her finger right on the sore spot: "The indignation of our literary theologians is comprehensible enough: Cummings's faults stand right out—indeed, what Eliotellus [*sic*] in eight years has not, for his graduation piece, permanently annihilated him?" Part of the trouble, she says, is that his faults are the faults of his virtues, and also that Anglophile critics have difficulty in accepting the influence of French poetry. Then she raises and answers four specific objections to Cummings. The first is that he fails in exact communication, and her reply is that poetry aims, not at "communication," but rather at "the perfect recreation of [the] experience in the reader." Second is that he is pretentious, to which she replies that boasting is a "classic poetic quality"—"*iactantia*"—and that Cummings' virtues are "gusto, abundance, magniloquence," and that in these "he is nearly unique." The question of bad taste is the third charge, which she resolves by distinguishing between good versus bad taste and taste versus no taste: Cummings has a lot of taste; "it is merely regrettable that some of it is bad." The last issue, excessive limitation of subject, is more serious, and she concedes that if Cummings does not develop beyond "spring, love and death," "he will remain, regrettably, a magnificent but minor singer." She opines, however, that his chances look good.

What Horton sees as the ossification of triviality and immaturity, Mangan sees as an inherent potential for growth, and the reason is that she can conceive of other poetic qualities than "knowledge, the chiefest instrument of evaluation and the essential means to maturity" (Horton)—qualities of liveliness, vividness, and immediacy—and therein lies a tale of utmost concern to students of the significance of modernism. Also, her "literary theologians" is a felicitous description, and we shall have occasion to return to it before we are done. Let us see what develops in the next fifteen years or so, before the publication of a second edition of collected poems.

IV

What we find during 1940–1953 is first, that the reviews seem to become generally more favorable; second, that his experimentalism is beginning to be more accepted and understood; and third, that his relation to traditionalism is becoming more and more evident. As Dendinger puts it, "While the debates about form are to continue, there is generally from 1938 on a quieter tone to the discussions." The period that encompassed the publication of 50 Poems (1940), 1 x 1 (1944), Xaipe (1950), and i:SIX NONLECTURES (1953) was to emerge as Cummings' major phase, in which, as Dendinger says, the "enfant terrible is being transformed into one of the foremost poets of the period, into a poet of the establishment. The prevailing tone of nostalgic acceptance of the prodigal in the 1953 reviews of the autobiographical i: six nonlectures [sic] would seem to indicate that the transformation was complete." His inclusion of Poems: 1923–1954 under that rubric, however, I question.

Although the reviews of 50 Poems contain some conventional carping, we also find some brilliant writing, such as these anonymous comments from the Santa Barbara News: after linking Cummings to Braque, Klee, and Kandinsky, and commenting on the modernist sense of the failure of common values, the reviewer says, "Each adventure to each art is innocent as sensibility is to phenomena and each onlooker must make his own pilgrimage." R. P. Blackmur, whose earlier strictures were being quoted favorably by many subsequent negative critics, amazingly says in the *Southern Review*, "I have been one of his admirers for twenty-one years since I first saw his poetry in the *Dial*," and adds, "There is . . . a sense of synergy in all the successful poems of Mr. Cummings." Then he concludes, "special attention should be called to the development of fresh conventions in the use of prepositions, pronouns, and the auxiliary verbs in the guise of substances, and in general the rich use of words ordinarily rhetorical . . . for the things of actual experience." And Theodore Spencer, writing in *Furioso*, says "the order of the poem [is] a reflection of the shape of the experience."

In reviewing *1 x 1* in the *Nation*, Marianne Moore writes that Cummings' book "is a thing of furious nuclear integrities." An anonymous reviewer in the *Providence Journal* calls Cummings "one of the liveliest, and one of the few, poets of our times." Spencer says, in the *New Republic*, "he has achieved a special depth of insight which few of his contemporaries can equal." Peter De Vries writes a very thoughtfully favorable review in *Poetry*. And so on.

The notices of *Xaipe*, beginning with Lloyd Frankenberg's in the *New York Times*, are similarly enthusiastic. Anonymous reviewers in the *Dallas News* and the *Providence Journal* are saying things like, "Cummings has been notably unsuccessful in hiding from his loyal if occasionally bewildered public that he is at heart a romantic and gifted, sensitive writer," and "within his range he has written some of the loveliest poetry in the language." Henry W. Wells says in *Voices*, "Both his manners and his technique are more disciplined." An anonymous writer in *Tomorrow* notices an increasing complexity of experience in this volume, and the miraculous way Cummings has of giving "seeming trivia their due life." David Daiches calls it in the *Yale Review*, "a rich and fascinating volume."

Of course, there are still a few cavils: Louise Bogan in the *New Yorker* notes "his deletion of the tragic" as a flaw; Rolfe Humphries in the *Nation* complains of a certain monotony; M. L. Rosenthal in the *New Republic* questions his apparent antisemitism; and Frederick Morgan in the *Hudson Review* wonders about the drastic simplification of vision. Morgan adds, "The extent to which one will be satisfied by Cummings' poetry . . . will in the long run depend on how wholeheartedly one is willing to subscribe to this attitude." I think it may also be partly whether one is willing to supply the missing portion of the context of his vision and art so as more adequately to understand it.

Not surprisingly, *i:SIX NONLECTURES*, in which, as the anonymous reviewer of the *Poet* says, "The bad bald poet tells all," seems to have gone a good deal of the way in that direction, for as we read from *Kirkus Reviews* and on through the unknown and known reviewers (the latter including Samuel F. Morse, Alfred Kazin, Charles Norman, William Saroyan, and Warner Berthoff), we find a practically unanimous chorus of praise. In writing for an actual audience in Sanders Theatre, Cummings seems to have found a more winning stance, reassuring his listeners that, although he still takes his individualism and artistic integrity very seriously, he is nevertheless devoted to wholesome, recognizable, and good-hearted human and poetic values.

Kazin, in fact, looks quizzically in the *New Yorker* at Cummings' "traditionalism": "He has always made a point of defying the Philistines, but at Harvard he stood up against our terrible century armed only with his memories and the Golden Treasury." Warner Berthoff, on the other hand and more tellingly, writing in the *New England Quarterly*, claims that Cummings has *avoided* the too-easy relapse into complacency characteristic of so many New England talents: "we meet [in Cummings] face to face the spectre of inverted gentility which since Thoreau has haunted the overbred New England writer. We meet him—and E. E. Cummings kills him again before our eyes." His weapon, Berthoff goes on to show, is his readings from "his own work and the Golden Treasury of lyric poetry to which he devoted the last third of each nonlecture." Here Cummings gives living proof of what he could only have "opinions" about in the prose of the nonlectures—his transcendent faith in art itself, and in the freshness and durability of his own art.

V

The romance is over, however, when *Poems: 1923–1954* comes out, and the whole battle fought in 1938 has to be fought all over again. Putting the poet's entire *oeuvre* together at that time into a single volume may have been a serious mistake, for instead of highlighting his growth in the eyes of modernist critics, it seems to have focused them back on his earlier limitations. Randall Jarrell's piece in the *New York Times Book Review* set an unfortunate tone: "He is a magical but shallow rhetorician," and "What I like least about Cummings' poems is their pride in Cummings and their contempt for most other people." Michael Harrington writes in *Commonweal* that "there is a serious lack of depth in Cummings' romanticism." John Ciardi says in the *Nation* that Cummings cannot see *relationships* between "good" and "bad," only their differences. G. S. Fraser in the *Partisan Review* emphasizes Cummings' lack of a tragic sense. Carl Bode in *Poetry* claims, "He is still a poet who is considerably more talked about than he deserves to be." Assuredly, a number of favorable reviews are to be found, chief among which are those by Samuel F. Morse, Paul Engle, and David Burns. But here, as before, we can best clarify the problem by studying in a bit more detail a pair of serious and extended opposing reviews.

Heading the case for the prosecution is Edwin Honig in the *Kenyon Review*. As have several other reviewers, he realizes this is a time for summing up, not only of Cummings but also of modernism itself. It is a time for comparative judgments. "Cummings' poetry contends less intrinsically with human values" than does that of Pound and Eliot, he says. "He doesn't thrive on paradox, like Eliot or Yeats." His techniques "often cloak attitudes that are cantankerous and juvenile." He believes that "only what acts *is*, and only what feels *is*; what merely thinks is not." In rebelling against the machine, his techniques make machines out of his poems, "a public confession of opposing selves." Cummings is an expressionist, and "Unlike his contemporaries he derives little from symbolism or imagism."

I would say, however, not only that Cummings is divided against himself, but also that modernism itself is. Such critics were having a problem with that part of modernism deriving from romanticism and analogous to certain forms of mysticism and orientalism—and, I might add, symbolism—the transcendental part which holds that there are higher forms of truth than those grasped by knowledge and intellect. I think the New Critics adopted a version of this notion, and then adapted it, under the influence of T. E. Hulme, Richards, and Eliot, to a version of the metaphysical tradition and emerged with a doctrine involving sinewy intellectuality, irony, "maturity," paradox, the tragic vision, et al. And it is precisely this latter doctrine which Cummings fails to exemplify.

As we have seen however, there are other and more inclusive ways to define modernism. John Logan in *Poetry*, arguing for the defense, begins by noting Cummings' compassion and his concern with self-transcendence, quoting from *i:SIX NONLECTURES*: "we should go hugely astray in assuming that art was the only self-transcendence. Art is a mystery: all mysteries have their source in a mystery-of-mysteries who is love." Logan comments: "we may note the connection between the notion of transcending ('climbing over') oneself and the notion of ecstasy ('standing outside'); the one follows the other: and without both there is neither love nor art." As far as "anti-intellectualism" is concerned, it "is basically an affirmation of the *mystery* of things," and a resistance against those "who insist on limiting the real and true to what they think they know or can respond to. . . . Cummings is directly opposed to letting us rest in what we believe we know; and this is the key to the rhetorical function of his famous language."

Logan then examines the charge that Cummings has failed to develop and refutes it point by point. Similarly, he reopens and reexamines the whole problem of the typographical experiments: dadaism, surrealism, and cubism share with the baroque "an interest in dissolving surfaces. Applied to poems, this means that they must not look as we *expect* poems to look." Nevertheless, the appearance of the poem is not an end in itself; it is, rather, a way of directing "the evocation of the poem in the mind of the reader," of expanding the connotative powers of language, and of bringing the reading under the control of the poet. All of which serves "to prevent the reader from resting in what he thinks he knows and what he expects."

It is surely one of the central doctrines of modernism in general, and not just the New Critical variety, that the work of art must be grappled with in and of itself and not by means of explanation and paraphrase. And it is surely one of the main justifications for such a doctrine that the nature of reality—especially our twentieth-century reality—is too complex to be grasped solely by intellection. In these terms, any modernist critic would have to admit Cummings into the fold. The split occurs when one branch of modernism, primarily the New Criticism, as I've been suggesting, wants to transcend the limits of intellection by complicating it with opposites set in tension, while the other branch wants to transcend intellection altogether in order to achieve a truly whole, pure, and nondualistic vision—an achievement more profound and more noble than the tragic vision itself.

Humanity's schools of thought and religion seem to fall characteristically into three divisions: there are those who try to arrive at the ultimate truth by means of churches, sacred texts, priests, and rituals; those who end up following these forms without any sense of their original purpose; and those who seek the truth apart from such forms, relying instead on their own direct contact with it. It might seem that this model explains Orthodox, Conservative, and Reform Judaism; Catholicism, Protestantism, and Puritanism; Hinduism, Buddhism, and Zen; and so on; but it often happens that within each branch itself there develop more formal and less formal tendencies. We seem to be dealing with basic conflicts which exist potentially in all of us, and splitting into factions rarely solves the problem. It is difficult to rely on our own direct contact with truth without feeling the need for forms; it is just as difficult to follow forms without losing a sense of direct contact with truth.

In terms of modernism, for example, I see the New Critical branch, because of its emphasis on knowledge, thought, and maturity, as containing our literary theologians, in Sherry Mangan's words; the antimodernists, because of their distrust of the unfamiliar, as containing our literary ritualists for the sake of ritual; and the antiritualists, because of their reliance on personal experience of the transcendent, as containing Cummings and the mystical tradition he embodies. But the problem is that these categories identify tendencies rather than separate schools. Thus the non-dualistic vision can be found in *parts* of Cummings, as it can be found in parts of Blake, Whitman, Yeats, Stevens—not to mention Coleridge, Wordsworth, Keats, Browning, Meredith, D. H. Lawrence, Woolf, and so on. And surely the strong strain of orientalism in much of modernism has significantly affected Yeats, Pound, and Eliot, for example, as well.

To call this vision "intuitive," "emotional," "childlike," "sentimental," "impulsive," "sensationalistic," "untragic," and so on, is to struggle vainly to define a unitary experience in the language of our dualistic tradition. And of course it is even more difficult to *achieve* than it is to find *language* for. That is the challenge and the burden of this branch of modernism. It is no wonder that many of Cummings' modernist critics resist it, and they have not been helped by his *own* resistance to it—in either case, a resistance no less strong than that of the conservative critics to modernism in general. In this sense, we can understand and accept all three, for there is a truth and a cogency to what each is trying to cope with and accomplish.

VI

A coda is in order for the reviews of 95 *Poems* (1958), the last book published before the poet's death, and hence the last one to be covered by Dendinger. Certain familiar key concerns recur throughout, almost as if there had not been an extended debate going on for over thirty-five years on these same points. John Logan in *Commonweal* notes, however, "In recent years Cummings has begun to be studied seriously and at length as an inventor, and there is a growing literature of research." Which reminds us pretty much of the limitations of book reviews, for their writers feel little obligation thoroughly to know what they are talking about or what others have said, relying primarily on their own deadlined reactions to the book before them. The well-worn sentence from Santayana, that to ignore the past is to be condemned to repeat it, comes handily to mind here.

Thus there is fresh puzzlement over Cummings' typographical and linguistic devices, and some head-scratching over whether he has developed or not. Three poems in particular tend to divide the critics: the oriental-looking typography of the opening poem describing the fall of a leaf, the invective of the poem satirizing Uncle Sam's indifference to the Hungarian fight for freedom, and the sentimentality of the "i am a little church" poem. As Sara H. Hays says in the *Pittsburgh Press*, "His audiences usually fall into two camps: those whose sensibilities are outraged and antagonized by his eccentricities, his verbal and typographical antics; and those who find these same characteristics fresh, exciting, significant, and the stuff of genius." Or, as W. G. Rogers points out in the *Charleston News and Courier*, "Cummings . . . is one of those contemporary creative figures who have managed to collect a small body of followers of utterly unshakable loyalty along with a wide public aware of their work but puzzled, disdainful or aloof."

Nevertheless, interestingly enough, the reviews included here favor Cummings by three to one. Let us look first at the naysayers, chief among whom are Paul Lauter, John Hollander, and W. D. Snodgrass. Lauter claims in the *New Leader* that Cummings' universe is so private that "we do not finally know what he is singing about." Hollander in the *Partisan Review* agrees "that Mr. Cummings' view of the world will no longer do." And Snodgrass in the *Hudson Review* sees him as a case "of arrested development." On the other hand, Philip Booth in the *Christian Science Monitor* asks, "And as for growing up, who wants to if we grow up beyond poems?" And Robert Graves claims in the *New York Times*, "Most poets slowly decay; Cummings slowly matures." Samuel F. Morse in the *Hartford Courant* praises the "staggering typography" as "a greater pleasure than ever." William Carlos Williams in the *Evergreen Review* likes Cummings' ear for American speech. Winfield Townley Scott—who has apparently gone through some changes—writing in the *Saturday Review*, proclaims that "Cummings has restored joy to poetry incomparably beyond any poet of our time." And Logan sums up: "Stevens is more genteel and gorgeous, Eliot more reflective and more religious, W. C. Williams more perfect in ear and cadence, Marianne Moore more academic and more precious, Pound more versatile and more outrageous, Frost more violent and more pastoral. But Cummings is the most provocative, the most sentimental, the funniest, the least understood."

That "understanding" is on its way, however, is shown most clearly by Anthony Wolff, writing in the *Daily Tar Heel* of the University of North Carolina. Cummings is difficult, he says, because he writes about the simplest things: "They are, essentially, Love and Being, themselves and inseparable, celebrated as epiphanies in each possible moment, and bitterly, sarcastically, angrily noted in their absence." This seems to me somewhat more than Dayton Kohler's praise in the *Louisville Courier-Journal* of Cummings' ability to "sense life with a child's senses," to sing of it "with a child's strong, clear voice." Wolff goes on: "And yet, though Love and Being are indeed the simplest things in life—are life itself—'mostpeople' find them difficult to apprehend. We are weaned from them, and it is often a difficult process to approach them again, especially as the moments of truth which they are for Cummings. Epiphanies are hard to come by."

Quite so. There is a lesson in here for all of us. It is not simply conservative reviewers who resist such awareness; it is also many modernist critics as well. And it is not merely these modernist critics; it is also Cummings himself. For he not only aimed at the highest vision, thereby provoking their ambivalence, but he also found it difficult to integrate his *own* ambivalence, thereby supplying them with ammunition against himself. But we are all in the same boat, and it behooves us to attempt a truer understanding of his faults by seeing them in the context of what he was truly aiming to do, thereby achieving for ourselves a fuller sense of life's possibilities in the context of which we can more fully understand our *own* faults. And that, in my proud and humble opinion—to borrow a phrase from Cummings—is what art and the criticism of art are all about.

9

Further Developments in Cummings Criticism, 1976–1979

Upon being asked by Linda Funkhouser and Daniel C. O'Connell, the editors of a special Cummings issue of *Language and Literature* (1984), to contribute something, I decided to continue my survey of Cummings criticism, this time focusing in depth upon a number of recent book-length publications. However, as the portion on Kennedy's *Dreams in the Mirror* seemed more appropriate for the third part of the present volume, I have edited the present chapter accordingly.

I

Herein is a sounding of the state of Cummings criticism in the late 1970s in which are examined four books published on the poet during the four years of 1976–1979. In focusing on these books, I find it useful, by way of providing a context for understanding better what was going on at that time, to attempt a brief sketch of the Cummings critical enterprise as a whole up to that point. First, the question of quantity: the total number of items on that poet, from 1922 to 1980, a span of almost sixty years, was well over a thousand, thus averaging almost twenty items a year. The picture by decades, however, is more revealing: the first three decades, 1922–1949, average roughly a hundred items each, while the second three, 1950–1980, average over two hundred items each—thus showing a significant increase which began in the 1950s. Cummings had published sixteen titles by then and twelve (including posthumous works) after. There was somewhat of a lag, then, as criticism caught up with him, but that seems entirely natural.

The question of quality is, of course, a more difficult matter to assess. Without putting too fine a point upon it, however, let me simply enumerate the names of some of the better-known literary, theater, and academic people who have written on Cummings: Jacques Barzun, Joseph Warren Beach, William Rose Benet, Eric Bentley, John Berryman, John Peale Bishop, R. P. Blackmur, Louise Bogan, John Malcolm Brinnin, Cleanth Brooks, Van Wyck Brooks, Kenneth Burke, Malcolm Cowley, Hart Crane, David Daiches, S. Foster Damon, Babette Deutsch, John Dos Passos, Elizabeth Drew, Max Eastman, Francis Fergusson, Leslie Fiedler, Dudley Fitts, F. Scott Fitzgerald, John Gould Fletcher, Ford Madox Ford, Robert Graves, Granville Hicks, Gilbert Highet, Stanley Hyman, Randall Jarrell, Howard Mumford Jones, Alfred Kazin, Hugh Kenner, Harry Levin, Marshall McLuhan, F. O. Matthiessen, Josephine Miles, Marianne Moore, John Middleton Murry, Octavio Paz, Roy Harvey Pearce, Ezra Pound, John Crowe Ransom, Kenneth Rexroth, Laura Riding, Karl Shapiro, Edith Sitwell, Theodore Spencer, Gertrude Stein, Allen Tate, Lionel Trilling, Robert Penn Warren, William Carlos Williams, Edmund Wilson, and Yvor Winters.

This is a fairly distinguished list of those whose attention Cummings has engaged. Yet several problems remain: one is that none has written a book on Cummings, and the other is that a significant number have written disparagingly about him. Not, to take up the former first, that a substantial number of books hasn't been written on Cummings. Beginning in 1946, there have been twenty-one separate volumes published to date—one in the 1940s, one in the 1950s, nine in the 1960s, and ten from 1970 to 1980.[1] Of these twenty-one items, two are special issues of journals devoted to the poet (*The Harvard Wake* and *Journal of Modern Literature*), two are bibliographies (Firmage and Rotella), four are pamphlets (Attaway, Triem, and the two Eckleys), two are collections of essays by various hands (Baum and Friedman), and therefore there remain eleven full-length critical and biographical studies (Norman, two Friedmans, Marks, Grossman, Wegner, Dumas, Fairley, Lane, Kidder, and Kennedy).

Admittedly, the quality of criticism is not necessarily dependent upon the fame of the critic, yet the fact that no luminaries have written a book on

Cummings is symptomatic of *something* significant. Think of some of the books on other modern writers: Harry Levin, Hugh Kenner, and Richard Ellmann on Joyce; Ellmann and John Unterecker on Yeats; F. O. Matthiessen and Stephen Spender on Eliot; Hugh Kenner on Pound; Frank Kermode and Helen Vendler on Stevens; Monroe Spears on Auden; Reuben Brower on Frost; William York Tindall and Elder Olson on Dylan Thomas; and so on. It's almost as if certain writers had a secure place in our literary canon *before* their interpreters came along, and therefore that some of our best critical talent felt safe in concentrating on them.

With Cummings, however, it has been otherwise: his very inclusion in our canon seems perpetually at issue, as we have seen, and not only have no noteworthies written a book about him, but also some have treated him negatively indeed—for example, Winters, Matthiessen, Blackmur, and Jarrell. Those who favor him, therefore, have tended to become defensive, as if needing to answer charges before going on with their work of analysis and interpretation.

The real significance, however, of some of the most recent work being done on Cummings is that we are beginning to see the results of the availability of his papers and letters, as well as of the publication of new scholarly aids and the development of new approaches. We now have a full-scale and objective biography, a new focus on individual poems and volumes of poetry, a better sense of his early career and of its relation to his later phase, and so on.

Let us, therefore, turn to the four volumes before us in the light of these introductory remarks.

II

First, the new secondary bibliographies, of which there are two. By far the most extensive is Rotella's. Published separately as a hardcover book, it is over two hundred pages in length, and it is particularly complete through 1975 or so but includes items up to 1977. It begins with a twenty-five-page introduction, which intelligently surveys and analyzes the critical trends decade by decade, and concludes with a very useful list of things remaining to be done: a selective edition of the best poems, a complete collection of letters, a concordance,[2] a study of Cummings' use of irony and ambivalence, of his personal sign system, of his treatment of death, his use of the city, his alleged solipsism, and his use of nature. He adds that the question of development needs further consideration, and that interdisciplinary studies using fresh critical methods should continue. He thinks that a more accurate appraisal of Cummings' place in modernism is desirable, and that the puzzle of his being frequently described as traditional in theme and modern in technique needs clarification. Most important, he believes, is the need for further studies of individual poems and groups of poems, for they would reveal his true importance in vision, craft, and development.

There follows a selected list of writings by Cummings, arranged chronologically, and then the secondary bibliography itself. This is arranged year by year, alphabetically by author within each year. Almost every item is described crisply and accurately, sometimes briefly, sometimes more extensively. Cross references are made for reprints and new editions. Everything is here: reviews, essays, chapters from books, books, significant references to Cummings in published letters and autobiographies, master's theses, doctoral dissertations, *Explicator* items, and so on. An attempt has been made to include foreign materials as well. The volume concludes with an extensive and useful index (the only complaint about the index I have is that significant names mentioned in the descriptions seem not to be indexed).

I cannot praise this book too much. It will surely become the standard reference for years to come, and I can only hope that Rotella will see fit to publish supplements in due course.[3] Any student of Cummings will be saved hours and days and weeks of busywork by consulting this volume; any student of Cummings' reception and reputation will find it indispensable; and any student of modern criticism will find it illuminating. There is now no longer any excuse for a critic, eminent or otherwise, to write as if only one view of Cummings were possible or sensible.

Artem Lozynsky's bibliography is a somewhat different affair, although good of its kind. Published as the conclusion to the special Cummings number of the *Journal of Modern Literature*, it is much more selective, running only to a bit more than 40 pages, although a little more up to date. While it is less than a quarter the length of Rotella's, however, it has about half as many items, most probably because his descriptions and cross-references are briefer. Having a short introduction, it is particularly useful in that it is arranged by categories rather than simply chronologically: bibliographies, books, general studies, individual works (divided further into reviews and commentaries), and individual poems. Within these selections it is arranged alphabetically by author. For someone looking for a given type of item, therefore, or for studies of given works or individual poems, this bibliography would be most useful. Limited by the exigencies of journal publication, it has of course, no index. Cross-checking Lozynsky's descriptions with those of Rotella for the same items would also prove useful to the student.

III

Let us consider the three new critical works next. The "E. E. Cummings Special Number" of the *Journal of Modern Literature*, guest-edited by Richard Kennedy, is best taken up first because it is, naturally, the most heterogeneous. As the first such special issue of a journal in thirty-three years, it presents an interesting contrast to the original *Harvard Wake* collection, which was guest-edited by José Garcia Villa. Since Cummings was still alive, of course, in 1946, he contributed three items of his own: a poem ("love our so right"), a fairy tale ("The Old Man Who Said 'Why'?"), and the entire *Santa Claus (A Morality)*. There follow fourteen mostly brief essays, and they are almost all by big names: Williams, Moore, Trilling, Levin, and so on. Basically, this is a collection of testimonials, with only a few slightly longer attempts at sustained analysis—by Spencer, Frankenberg, and Gregory and Zaturenska. Then there is a list of Cummings' publications to date, and nine unrelated contributions by Stevens, Aiken, Williams, and so on. The whole journal is under one hundred pages.

JML, on the other hand, has seven major essays by academics—the shortest is eleven pages, and the longest is thirty-six pages—plus previously unpublished poems and documents, plus Lozynsky's bibliography. The whole comes to over two hundred pages—all of which is indicative of the changes in Cummings criticism during these thirty-three years, but not more so than the contents themselves. The first essay is by Kennedy on "The Emergent Styles, 1916," which appeared shortly thereafter as a chapter in his full-length biographical study, and which we'll discuss at some length in chapter 12 below.

The second is by Irene Fairley, "Cummings' Love Lyrics: Some Notes by a Female Linguist." Essentially a continuation of the work she began in her 1975 book, this article argues that, although some of Cummings' attitudes toward women are offensively stereotypical, they are less so when embodied via his charged distortions of linguistic conventions than when expressed more straightforwardly. He is best, of course, she concludes, when attitudes which are not offensive are expressed deviantly. Two valid and significant problems are being raised here: one about the relationship between theme and technique, which we recall that Rotella defined as important, and the other about the nature of Cummings' attitudes toward women. It is to the second that I want to direct our attention for a moment.

I will not deny that there is something problematic about Cummings' treatment of women in his writing, but I would like to question the way Professor Fairley handles it. She first notices the problem in his polarization of women into the two usual sexual extremes of whore and maiden. His portraits of prostitutes are degrading, while his idealized image of woman is collectivized and depersonalized—in either case, Woman is seen as object rather than as individual. And she finds this to be true for Cummings both early and late, despite the fact that other critics have claimed his treatment of love becomes less sexual and more transcendental as he matures. For the early phase, she quotes Gregory and Zaturenska in support, who say some of the women in Cummings' poems resemble those in the fiction of Hemingway and Dos Passos: these "young women . . . were mindless, and were articulate only when they were performing their ultimate and primary functions within the embraces of their lovers."

Now the trouble with this description is that it is *itself* a stereotype—lost generation and all that. Whereas a close look at Hemingway's Lady Brett, for example, would reveal that she is less either whore or maiden than independent woman, and that her "promiscuity" is at least as much a comment on the male macho mystique as it is an expression of her female bitchiness and despair. But whatever else she is, she does not impress me as "mindless." Yet Fairley gets rather tangled up in that word when she applies it back to Cummings' "you shall above all things be glad and young" (*New Poems*, #22, in the 1938 *Collected Poems*), where, she says, the speaker "directs his woman to remain mysteriously the eternal, enticing, Feminine . . . stressing the difference and distance between the sexes." And she concludes: "The mindlessness that he advises makes the stereotype all the more offensive, despite the fact that he prescribes the same handicap for himself."

Handicap? Whatever else we may think of Cummings' vision of transcendence—and we shall have to take this up again further on also—we can never say that he considers it a handicap. It is one thing for Man to put Woman on a pedestal so that he may keep her safely out of the way of his important business in life—kicking Her upstairs, so to speak—but it is quite another to scorn, as Cummings surely does, that "important business" and to look to Woman for Man's redemption into a truer and more vital vision of life.

But the really confusing thing in Fairley's argument is that she goes on to *praise* his transcendental view of love in another context. Apparently, when he shifts his focus from his lady to the lovers as a unit, his transcendentalism becomes acceptable. In "if up's the word;and a world grows greener" (95 *Poems*, #95), for example, he "expresses . . . the transcendental qualities . . . characteristic of the later poems." "In these works," she continues, "Cummings provides a more philosophical grounding for the male-female relationship than what we find in the early 'i like my body when it is with your' [*&* (*AND*), 218], yet he still retains all of his play with language, challenging the reader." It is very difficult for me, however, to see any significant difference on this point between "you shall above all things" (1938) and "if up's the word" (1958): if the earlier poem has the speaker asking the lady to be transcendental so that he may learn from her, while the later has him asking her to join him in seeking transcendence, the value-concept remains the same. We read in the former, "that you should ever think,may god forbid / . . . for that way knowledge lies," while in the latter we read, "in even the laziest creature among us / a wisdom no knowledge can kill is astir."

The significant differences I do see are, first, the different position, already noted, that the speaker assumes vis-à-vis the lady; and second, the somewhat more complex view of transcendence in the later piece. These poems are separated by twenty years, yet I would think the earlier one would be more acceptable to a contemporary feminist rather than less, in that the relationship implied is more reciprocal—the speaker has something to ask and something to receive—whereas in the later he explains and invites. *Both*, however, state or suggest union. As for the second difference, the later poem does not simply oppose knowledge and love, as does the earlier, but rather brings in the third term, "wisdom," to effect a more integrated reconciliation. One could, if one wished, claim that this is a "more philosophical" way to relate to a woman than in terms of "mindlessness," but I don't think this really makes all that difference in the context of Cummings' whole work—especially when one recalls that "mindlessness" is an honorific term for him and means pretty much the same thing as "wisdom."

So we see here a curious problem: on the one hand, new ways of analyzing Cummings' stylistic devices and of using these tools to relate theme and technique in new ways; and on the other, the question of whether new ways, however sharp, can be of much use when the theme part of Cummings is being misread and distorted to begin with. No matter, that is, how keen is our sense of the parts, that sense will help very little unless our sense of the whole poem—and of the whole *oeuvre*—is even keener. This ability can be taught, developed, and improved by analysis, and it can be tested by analysis, but I do not think it can be *replaced* by analysis. We must try to hold the whole poem in our minds at once as we talk about its parts and devices, and we must try to make our interpretation of these parts and devices accord with our sense of the whole; simultaneously, as our view of the parts and devices becomes clearer, our sense of the whole may shift toward more inclusiveness. I am describing, of course, what has been called the hermeneutic circle, except that I don't think it's simply a circle. First of all, our sense of the relation between parts and whole can be tested (by means of the criteria of economy, coherence, completeness, and so on); and second, our basic sense of the whole comes from our immersion in the author, our surrender, however temporary, to his vision, our willingness to listen—and do our homework.

It seems to me that the third essay in *JML*, "Acoustical Rhythms in 'Buffalo Bill's,'" by Linda Bradley Funkhouser, is an even clearer illustration of this problem. Professor Funkhouser's basic premise is that "empirical evidence," by which she means measuring the pace according to which different readers, including the poet himself, read the poem aloud, can help us choose among varying interpretations of the poem. The middle term of this argument is simply that meaning and tone in some way are dependent upon pause, pace, energy, and rhythm of reading. Her chief finding is that Cummings recites the poem more slowly than either her subject group (ten professors of literature) or her control group (ten inexperienced readers), and that this supports the interpretation of the poem as a satire on Buffalo Bill as just another fake commercialized American "hero." The claim is that the special slowness of Cummings' reading of the concluding lines strongly suggests irony and sarcasm.

Well, this may be so, but I have always felt that the irony and satire were directed against "Mister Death" rather than Bill—against Death in the sense that Bill is still too much alive to handle. The earlier "defunct," about which the critics who see Bill satirized have made much ado, seems to me to be ironic in the sense of saying, yes, now Bill's body is inert, an empty lump of dirt, but his skill, energy, and beauty are immortal. The beginning "defunct," in other words, is an exaggeration which makes the concluding denigration of Death (and implied celebration of Bill) that much more intense by contrast.

There are various reasons why I prefer my interpretation—the emphasis in the middle part of the poem is, after all, on Bill's skill; Cummings was both early and late an admirer of such skill; the complexities and ironies called for by the other interpretation do not seem to be actually in the poem, nor would they be characteristic of Cummings' usual approach or of his usual objects of satire; and so on—but the point is not which is correct. The point is that the "empirical evidence" here presented at such great length and in such patient detail cannot in and of itself determine whether the concluding sarcasm is directed at Bill or at Death. That requires, as I have been saying, a sense of the whole poem and of the whole Cummings. Of course, we may disagree about this sense, but we cannot settle things simply by looking at parts and devices, no matter how closely.

The fourth article, Edith A. Everson's "E. E. Cummings' Concept of Death," is more in the line of tracing certain words and attitudes through-out the *oeuvre* in an effort to do justice to the complexity of the poet's vi-sion. Basically pinning her interpretation on an analysis of *Santa Claus* and "dying is fine)but Death" (*Xaipe*, #6)—interestingly, she does not take up the Buffalo Bill poem—she sorts out the various positive and negative meanings which Cummings attaches to the concept of death, and relates these meanings to Cummings' concepts of love, sex, nature, knowledge, commercialism, and so on. Most significantly, she points out that Cummings does not regard dying "as the doorway to another conscious existence," and she quotes the following from the published letters: eternity means "not time-adinfinitum, but time-lessness." He does not value a future life, but what he calls an "illimitable now," an unbounded possibility for growth in the present life.[4] This distinction will become more important as we pro-ceed. Professor Everson's essay is sensitive work, corresponding to another of Rotella's suggestions, and it points the way toward further exploration.

The fifth article, "Cummings and Cubism: The Influence of the Visual Arts on Cummings' Early Poetry," by Rushworth Kidder, is, like several others Professor Kidder has published in this vein, a groundbreaker, and I hope he will manage to get this work published in book form.[5] The issue here is not so much Cummings' paintings and drawings, however, as his "bringing into poetry the many advances which, through Cubism, Futurism, and other developments in art, had radically altered visual taste in the first decades of this century." And Kidder makes that essential distinction between Apollinaire, the Dada poets, and so on, who "strive to make visual art out of words in much the same way a draftsman makes a picture out of lines," as opposed to Cummings, who "always made *poetry* out of words." Then, examining some of the poet's early prose writings, he emerges with two basic ideas about art which Cummings was considering at the time: that art should focus on the "moment"—on an action in the process of change—and that it should represent not the object but the way the artist sees the object. Kidder views these ideas as forming an unresolved tension in Cummings' mind between realism and abstraction and proceeds to examine Cummings' early art work in the light of this tension.

The basic question then becomes how Cummings' artistic theory and practice affected his poems. We are dealing, Kidder recognizes, with the vexed question of the parallels among the arts, and he distinguishes between superficial and meaningful parallels. Simply referring to the visual arts—by words that name colors, by poems that present painterly scenes, by poems *about* painting and painters, and by comments on visual art's techniques—as Cummings sometimes does, does not actually import "into the realm of literary composition the aesthetics of the visual arts." It is merely to use art as a subject matter.

On the other hand, meaningful parallels are found in the formal features—selection and arrangement of materials to achieve form—common to all the arts but which distinguish the arts from the other pursuits and products of man. Kidder chooses to discuss three formal features common to both Cummings' painting as well as his poetry: fragmentation and fusion, simultaneity, and bilateral symmetry. The way he works these features out in relation to the painting and the poetry has to be read to be fully appreciated, and he concludes with the interesting observation that, as Cummings' art became less abstract by the end of the twenties, his poetry became more so, as if he were still trying to balance that unresolved tension. Yet Cummings stands almost alone, he adds, among modern poets in his attempts to relate the two arts thus meaningfully and organically.

The sixth article is a brief reading of "morsel miraculous and meaningless" (*No Thanks*, #71) from a Catholic perspective, by Valerie Meliotes Arms. While I have no doubt that Cummings absorbed some Unitarian religiosity from his father and some Catholic religiosity from his third wife, Marion Morehouse, I cannot help but feel that any worshipful and reverential feeling and imagery we may find in his writings stems more from his own special brand of transcendentalism than from anything specifically Christian, and that he was more influenced by Lao-tzu than by Plato—a point I have mentioned before and shall have to take up again below.

The next essay contains my own analysis of Cummings' posthumously published works, which comprises chapters 2 and 10 herein and which represents an attempt to round out my extended interpretation of his *oeuvre* as a whole.

This concludes the criticism portion of *JML*. There follow, in addition to the aforementioned bibliography, a collection of twenty unpublished poems by Cummings as well as the earliest versions of four others, presented by George Firmage; documents from the Richard Norton papers concerning the Ambulance Corps in World War I, presented by Marte Shaw of the Houghton Library; and information and documents concerning La Ferté-Macé, presented by J. P. Vernier of the University of Rouen.

All in all, this is a very useful, if somewhat miscellaneous and uneven, volume, establishing, however tentatively, several beachheads and deepening our push into more well-known territories.

IV

Gary Lane's *I Am: A Study of E. E. Cummings' Poems* appeared three years before *JML*, but I want to take it up here, in combination with Kidder's book-length study, as representing extended single-critic approaches falling within the stated time frame. This is a modest, slender volume, barely over one hundred pages long. Essentially a semiclose reading of twenty-five poems, it divides them up, after an introduction, into five thematic groups of five poems each. Thus Lane strives for the advantages of both depth and breadth. The first two explicative chapters deal with two aspects of love — seduction and selfhood — the second two with two kinds of death (compare Everson's piece discussed above) — true and false — while the fifth deals with the final unity of transcendental growth. The problem I have with this book, however, is that it is neither deep nor broad, falling somewhere in between.

In terms of its interpretive scheme, it has very little that is new to offer, being based, essentially, on the old lyric-satire dialectic which has cramped Cummings criticism from the beginning. Nor does it have anything that is particularly fresh to say about Cummings' themes and attitudes, speaking of transcendence this and transcendental that as if everything were perfectly clear. In terms of its analyses, although Professor Lane would have us believe that only a few of the poems he discusses have received previous explicative attention — none as detailed as his — and that his is the first study to make use of the poet's published letters, it is with amazement that we realize that he can devote less than four pages apiece, on the average, to each poem.

And we do not find anything exceptional in the analyses themselves, however short or long: he simply explains what the poem is about and then proceeds to correlate this with its technical and stylistic devices, tying the whole in with the theme of its particular group. He is cheerful, not to say cheery; he writes gracefully, if a bit preciously at times; and although he speaks here and there of Cummings' faults and limits, he belongs basically to the adulatory school. While answering to that need Rotella spoke of for work on individual poems, this book only begins to fulfill it. It is hard to know what audience it was written for.

Answering to the same need, Kidder's *E. E. Cummings: An Introduction to the Poetry*, is a somewhat different matter. Proposed frankly "as a reader's guide to individual poems," it is a poem-by-poem, book-by-book account of the entire poetic corpus. And its special virtue is that it often considers an individual poem in terms of its neighbors in a given book, as well as of its place in the book as a whole, making capital of the fact that Cummings paid careful attention to the arrangements of his volumes. Furthermore, not only does Kidder make actual use of Cummings' published letters, he also has consulted the unpublished material as well. And he concludes with a bibliographical appendix listing other analyses of individual poems, volume by volume. Of the nine book-length, single-author critical studies of Cummings extant at the time, this one filled a need which none of the others did. It is in the objective mode, moreover, conveying a healthy sense of Cummings' concern to write highly wrought and organized poems despite his professed objections to "thinking," and of his ability to tell the difference between sentiment and sentimentality.

I do, however, have two complaints. The first has to do with the very nature of the book itself: a poem-by-poem account makes for difficult reading, and it seems less like a critical study than a reference work. Although the analytical part of this book is just over two hundred pages or so, it seems hardly adequate for the job and is rather crowded. Other reader's guides to other poets are significantly longer.

My other complaint is rather more substantive. Kidder makes as much out of the Christian elements, à la Professor Arms, as possible, and then some. In discussing "one's not half two. It's two are halves of one" (*1 x 1*, #16), for example, he says "Cummings here takes over an ideal central to Christian monotheism: that oneness, 'the song which fiends and angels sing,' is the salient attribute of Deity." Then, at the end of the book, he speaks of love as Cummings' main subject, and of how it evolved from romantic and sexual emphases to "a purified and radiant idea, unentangled with flesh and worlds, the agent of the highest transcendence. It is not far, as poem after poem has hinted, from the Christian conception of love as God. It is this sense of God that Cummings' poems of praise celebrated, this sense that his satires have sought to protect. It is this sense that Cummings, whose entire body of work is finally an image of himself, would have us see as the source of his own being."

Well, this is strange! Or again, Kidder, in speaking of "life is more true than reason will deceive" (1 x 1, #52), although almost seeming to be making another point entirely, pulls the chestnut out of the fire at the last minute. Quoting "the mightiest meditations of mankind / canceled are by one merely opening leaf," he draws attention to the line which follows, "beyond whose nearness there is no beyond." While indicating that he understands this to refer to Cummings' sense of the here and now—what he himself discussed in *JML* in relation to art focusing on the "moment," and what I see as Cummings' Taoist sense—he nevertheless comments: "Reversing the expected conception of obsolete pasts and unborn futures, he provides the paradox that introduces his main, and quite Christian, point: 'here less than nothing's more than everything.' Not surprisingly, the poem moves in its final couplet to a consideration of what Paul called 'the last enemy that shall be destroyed' (I Cor. 15:26). Death, here, is seen as a merely relative term, a conception, for 'death, as men call him, ends what they call men.' Beauty, however, survives by its omnipresence the mere temporality of dying."

Now I may be greatly mistaken, but I do not think you can have any kind of Christianity based on the sense that organismic process is all that there is and that this is indeed sufficient. I will grant that Cummings was in some ways a Christian. I will grant that there are some elements in Christianity which are similar to this element in Taoism—"Cast your bread upon the waters" comes to mind as an example. And I will even grant that Cummings himself was sometimes confused about this distinction, as I have mentioned. But I cannot grant that a leaf with no beyond, whose nothing is more than everything, makes a "quite Christian point." What Cummings means by "nothing" here is not specifically Christian at all, as is also suggested by Professor Everson.

The poem as a whole is built on a series of contrasts, with "beauty" at the center: "life" is truer than reason, more secret than madness, deeper than lose, higher than have; but "beauty" is even truer, more secret, deeper, higher. "Beauty," epitomized by leaf and bird—that is, natural process—is greater than mankind's mightiest meditations, makes futures obsolete, pasts unborn. It is at this point that the poet says "here," "here less than nothing's more than everything." Continuing the basic contrast-series on which the poem is structured, "nothing" means "beauty," and "everything" means those things which life is more than, and it means "life," which "beauty" is more than.

What we have here, in other words, is a way of escalating superlatives, and the paradox is that at its center beauty is made most superlative by being belittled (compare the lovers as "anyone" and "noone" in "anyone lived in a pretty how town" [50 *Poems*, #29])—"one *merely* opening leaf," "some *littler* bird," and "*less* than nothing"—which simply indicates the speaker's awareness that what men consider important, such as abstractions, is really unimportant, and what men consider unimportant, such as a leaf or a bird, is really of the utmost importance. "Nothing," then, as it so often does in Cummings, refers ironically to the alive awareness of the here and now without our usual concerns about clocks and calendars, our hopes and fears, our memories and plans, our ideas and attempts at control. As "no-where" equals "now/here," so too does "nothing" equal "no/thing"—that is, a universe of aliveness as opposed to an unworld of thingness.

The concluding couplet returns to the opening contrast: there beauty was more than life, here it is more than death. Although death ends men— that is, life—"beauty is more now than dying's when"—that is, the time-lessness of the present moment outlives timebound things, which have be-ginnings and endings, pasts and futures. To be truly in the moment is to experience timelessness, eternity, heaven, transcendence—call it what you will, but it is quite a different awareness of eternity, heaven, and so on, from that expressed by Christianity, despite similarities in attitude and language. And it is also quite a different awareness of the moment from that espoused by the carpe diem philosophy, which Kidder also mistakenly sees running throughout Cummings' poems. To be alive in the moment is not hedo-nism either, for to be alive in the moment means to experience all the pro-cess of existence, not just the "pleasurable" ones. Indeed, as the organismic philosophy says, and as Cummings agrees, pleasure and pain are merely surfaces, a set of abstractions created by man's fatal need to divide and con-quer natural process (50 *Poems*, #43). As life and death are not opposed states but rather parts of the same system, so too are pleasure and pain. The process—beauty—includes and supersedes them all.

This, or something like this, is what I mean by reading a poem in terms of the whole—the whole of Cummings as well as of the poem—and it is because this is what Kidder sometimes does so well that I have taken the trouble to counteract an unfortunate tendency on his part to Christianize Cummings beyond reason. Indeed, I suspect that he has only an imprecise apprehension of what "now" and "nothing" really mean in Cummings; I suspect that very few of his other critics, whether positive or negative, have a very clear sense of these central terms in Cummings either. It is a kind of awareness Cummings himself struggled all of his life to achieve; it is a kind of awareness we must all struggle with if we are to have any sense of it; and it is the kind of awareness without which we cannot really understand or appreciate either Cummings' achievements or his limitations in any very specific manner. The truth seems to be that we can only truly understand anything—not by simply going into it—but more by going into *ourselves*.

part

three

:the

writer

10

Cummings Posthumous II

The Letters

In this section we focus on the writer as a person, without forgetting, however, the importance of this inquiry in helping us understand the writer. Although the present chapter originally appeared in the *Journal of Modern Literature* for 1979 as part of my study of the posthumous works presented in chapter 2, it clearly belongs here in terms of the organization of this book. I must say that *Selected Letters*, edited in 1969 by Dupee and Stade, was my first real inkling of the extent to which Cummings himself was able to analyze his own inner problems and ambivalences, and as such, along with Kennedy's biography, opened up a whole new—and difficult—area of inquiry for me.

I

Although I want to direct attention to certain of Cummings' inner conflicts as they appear in the letters, I will begin by noting a few of their features that seem directly interesting and pertinent in terms of the more public side of the writer.

F. W. Dupee and George Stade, the editors of the letters, say in their foreword that Cummings "seems not to have regarded letter writing as . . . a conscious art," although "the survival of the first and second drafts of a number of his letters testifies to the care he used when he wanted to" (xv). They mention later that he "normally made and preserved carbons" of his letters from 1947 on (xviii). It seems to me that the latter two remarks are more indicative than the first of what the reader finds in this volume. My impression is that they were very carefully written indeed, for when Cummings sat down to write, he was a writer—no matter what it was he was writing. Dupee and Stade concede the point a bit grudgingly: "Insofar as conscious art is detectable in his letters it is recognizably akin to the art of his verse and prose, since he was as thoroughly all of a piece as any fine and celebrated poet has ever been" (xv).

Cummings generally has three prose styles: the careful and deliberate balance found in "A Foreword to Krazy" (1946) or *i:SIX NONLECTURES* (1953), for example; the zany linguistic hijinks found in *No Title* (1930) and some of the satirical essays, for example; and the ecstatic lyricism of the latter part of the introduction to the 1938 *Collected Poems* and parts of *Eimi* (1933), for example. And the reader of *Selected Letters* will find elements of the same styles here, but of particular note are the many letters—especially to Ezra Pound—falling into the second category that are so full of surrealistic puns and verbal streams of consciousness that they become well-nigh cryptic. Pound himself, in fact, appears to have had some difficulty in deciphering them! (204–5).

The second public feature is the interesting record of his literary friendships and tastes, and of his remarks about and explications of his own writings—as well as his general comments about art. In addition to Pound, he knew and corresponded with William Carlos Williams, Edmund Wilson, Allen Tate, A. J. Ayer, Archibald MacLeish, Marianne Moore, John Dos Passos, Kenneth Burke, John Peale Bishop, and Robert Graves. He also knew Hart Crane, Malcolm Cowley, and Max Eastman. He makes interesting comments on Gertrude Stein, T. S. Eliot, Céline, Dinesen, Yeats, Dylan Thomas, Santayana, Swinburne, Rilke, Jeffers, Jung, Freud, Thoreau, Blake, Browning, Mann, Joyce, and Lawrence. Of particular value are his reluctant interpretations of his own works when pressed by an importunate reader, and I found of interest his many struggles with printers, editors, publishers, producers, directors, and translators to get his writings before the public properly. Also important are his many comments about art, especially his preference for representational painting and respect for traditional grammar and conventional poetic forms.

These letters are carefully if not deliberately written, then, and they contain a strong public component. As Dupee and Stade reassure us, Cummings "seems not to have regarded letter writing as . . . a vehicle for any urgent confessional impulse . . . he seldom soars to any heights of sustained introspection or plunges into any depths of mere personal scandal, about himself or anyone else" (xv). Furthermore, as they also explain, the letters we have here have been pretty thoroughly winnowed: they have printed only about one-fourth of the total number they recovered (265 out of a thousand or so). Additionally, as the editors inform us, Cummings' first and second wives—Elaine Thayer and Anne Barton—no longer had any communications that he may have addressed to them. And finally, since this volume was published just before Marion Morehouse, the poet's third wife, died, we can be sure that nothing that might have reflected negatively on Cummings could have possibly gotten through.

II

None of this sort of selectivity is to the point, however, since that kind of privacy is not at issue. I want to deal with the whole problem of conflicts going on inside him which do not find expression in the poetry—or if they do, are pretty well disguised—and which he is only intermittently aware of and only rarely able to integrate, and to trace the course of these conflicts as they work their way through his personal life in the world and leave their mark upon the inner structure of his emotional and intellectual life as well. My hope is to place the writings and career in this broader context and, by appreciating what was selected out as well as what was included in, to achieve a greater understanding of their ultimate significance. I once wrote that Cummings (like Whitman) created an artistic persona and then transformed the man into that persona so that they became one (*E. E. Cummings: The Art of His Poetry*, chapter 1) and we could have guessed at what it must have cost. Now we can have a better idea of that price. Indeed, we can have a clearer idea of the slippage which any such attempt must have incurred between man and mask.

First there is an extremely telling ambivalence, as a young man, toward his parents—which we have already noted above in chapter 5, and about which Richard Kennedy has much to say, as we shall see, in his biography. Between the ages of twenty-three and twenty-nine (1917–1923), when he was in the French prison of *The Enormous Room* (1922) and then in an Army camp at Fort Devens, and later when he was settling in New York, Cummings evinced quite a desire to be free of his family's influence and help — even urging Elizabeth, his younger sister, to follow suit. "I see the thing thru, alone, without any monocled Richards, American ambassadors, or anything else," he writes from France in 1917 (40). Apparently his father was offering to wield his considerable influence and obviously did later, as we learn from *The Enormous Room*. His father also seems to have wondered why Estlin accepted conscription instead of a commission in the army, and the son answers, "Mine is the perspiration of my own existence, and that's all I give a proper and bloody damn for" (51), and "if my prodigal family wants to keep on best terms with its fatted calf, it will lease the pasture the calf wants to graze in. For even a calf has a will of its own, they say!" (53). Already the self-conscious artist, he affirms the artist's need to know life at first hand (52). After the war, in 1920, Cummings briefly planned a sea voyage (which he never took), and rejected his father's concern once more: "in short, you will let me go my own way in my flannel shirt and my ideas" (72).

But these rebellious sentiments are mild in comparison to his advice, during 1922–1923, to his kid sister Elizabeth, who was apparently thinking of moving to New York also. After telling her to be independent and to trust her feelings, he says she won't be able to do these things "until you have KNOCKED DOWN AND CARRIED OUT all *the* teach*a*ble swill of Cambridge etc. And I'm the nigger that knows it and is sympathetic to you for that reason;because *my mind has been there too*. . . . To hell with everything which tries,no matter how kindly,to prevent me from LIVING MY OWN LIFE — KINDNESS,always,is MORE DANGEROUS than anything else!!" (86). Or again: "to inhabit the amiable and succulent bosom of one's relations not to mention one's family is to—I use [R. Stewart] Mitchell's momentous words,borrowed from St. Paul—'die daily'" (94). And finally: "I am glad you are reading smutty books,living in New York,drinking gasolene coctails [*sic*], etc. A sister to be proud of" (102).

Cummings, of course, does take a few shots at Cambridge in his published writings, but he never hints at the suffocation he felt in growing up in his family or at the difficulty he felt in breaking free of its influence. He was favored and encouraged by his parents, and this accounts for his public piety and reverence. But he also seems to have felt that along with his parents' approval came a tacit set of values, and that these values interfered with his individuality and growth as an artist. There is, naturally, that nor-

mal part of maturing which requires separation and independence, but there
is also a suggestion, as we shall see in a moment, that Cummings felt he
was *different* from his father and needed to protect that difference. His father, as we shall also see, in addition to having the vitality and versatility
and warmth which Cummings publicly celebrated, was the head and support of a family, a minister, a professor, a social scientist, and reformer—
quite a proper, progressive, and intellectual citizen, and as such he must
have represented on some level many of the things Cummings felt he had
to dissociate himself from.[1] This explains his rebelliousness, but we have
already puzzled over why he chose not to deal more explicitly with it in his
published writings.

Whatever the answer may be, I do think this dilemma in part underlies
his characteristic later stance as the beleaguered New England eccentric,
as we shall see below, and is in part accounted for by the unfortunate result
that he did not actually succeed in freeing himself from his family's influence after all. He tried, finally, to get a hardship discharge from the Army
(55–56), and he characteristically needed and received money from home
between 1920 and 1939 (74, 82, 110, 123, 127, 142–43, 147). A very poignant
burst of dependency came in 1925 (when he was almost twenty-nine), after
Elaine, his first wife, left him, and he was seeking visitation rights to
their daughter: "It seems to me that father's brains(which I have ever
admired,unlike my own)plus the life which he has given to society in the
economic sense of the word ought to rise up,here,and somehow . . .
magnificantly Save The Day before it's too late—mind you,he may know a
Boston lawyer who's a genius;and anyway,he is a famous man whereas I am
a small eye poet" (108–9).

III

I have suggested that Cummings, having started off in a blaze of youthful
vigor and independence, became deeply hurt by the failure of his first marriage and by the fact that he could not make a go of it by himself in his
career. Surely such disappointment was sufficient for the development of a
lifelong sense of disparity between himself and most of the rest of the world.
And, indeed, he was fortunate in finding in the Sibley Watsons, who were
always supporters, a substitute for his family during his middle and later
years. Having received intermittent moral and financial help from Watson
during the twenties, thirties, and forties (133, 188, 195), Cummings finally

made a formal request at the beginning of 1950: "perhaps you can help me. I cannot see how to go on unless am sure of 5000\$ [*sic*] a year." And then he goes on to spell out his budgetary picture, offering Joy Farm [Cummings' summer place in Silver Lake, New Hampshire, inherited from his parents] as security if need be (202).

There is something rueful in all this, especially in the light of the fact that Cummings *wanted* to be self-supporting. Eleven years previously, in 1939, he had written to Watson, "thank you most kindly for the 300 and am literally American enough to hope I'll be able to 'make my own way' 'some day' 'soon.' Seem to remember mon père telling me the best thing which could happen to you would be that what you want to do most should give you a living;anyhow,feel this is so" (148–9).

*   *   *

And yet, despite his disappointment and the fact that he had infinite difficulty in making his own way, he spoke early and late of self-sufficiency in the face of failure, of his proud independence, of his own defiant scorn of security, and of the virtue of suffering as a gift. Somehow his early need for freedom still had to be fulfilled. How could he do this? Shift the terms of the conflict: not being able to be *economically* independent, he felt that *spiritual* freedom was a superior virtue. Trying to cheer Stewart Mitchell up in 1920 for the latter's feelings of failure, Cummings says, "only,I quietly insist,my worship of and my confidence in my*Self* is unmitigated in the face of these *paltry*(ourword,Monsieur)Thermopolae" (74). In 1948 he writes to another friend, "concerning uncertainty(alias insecurity,or whatever mostpeople fear)I rather imagine that insofar as an artist is worth his spiritual salt he can never get enough" (186). And in 1956, writing to Mrs. Watson, he mentions some notebooks of his "(whereof 200&some already exist)" and quotes some passages he had written therein nine years before: "all fear is an ignorance of the truth that what we call 'suffering' or 'pain' or 'sorrow' (or 'evil') is a great gift. . . . [and]'if you turn the other cheek truly,' something happens which makes you invulnerable & and your wouldbe foe powerless" (249–50).

Certainly Cummings experienced enough anxiety and deprivation to qualify him for making those statements, and his letters from his fortieth year on speak recurringly of his difficulties, his lack of money, the hostility of the critics, the lack of attention given to his painting, etc. (142, 147, 202, 252, 263). He quotes admiringly, in 1959, near the end of his life, from Isak

Dinesen: "and so I learned that,if you have no faith,if you are quite without hope,and if you do just a very little,and then a little more,and again still more,it will all of itself become something" (261). And his letters from age forty-seven on also speak frequently of his arthritis, his thinning hair, his fear of travel, his stage fright, his feelings of tension, and so forth (163, 189, 195, 211, 238, 245).

But without self-pity, blaming, complaining, or bitterness. He could do without these props. Nevertheless, not many can stand naked in the void, and he did need a defense system: the compensatory image he built of himself as taking a lonely stand against a noncomprehending world did the job. Feeling his family's love as an encroachment, and yet needing it, he concluded that his individuality required vigilant protection; launching himself confidently against the world to make a career as an artist and yet finding himself bruised and impoverished, he inferred that he was the champion of values no one else believed in—except himself, fiercely, and a few friends and admirers such as the Watsons. They could give him familial support—both financial and moral—without the importation of well-meaning values to be resisted: "how wonderful! You-&-Sibley understand me:understand that I'm perfectly helpless unless I'm loved by people whom I can respect—understand that such people are very much rarer than rarest," he writes to Mrs. Watson in 1948 (188). Someone with a life-dream may need others to believe in it in order to feel real, but that's not the same thing as being independent—it's merely a shift from one sort of family to another to depend on.

IV

The result from his mid-forties on is the pride of the "101% New Englander" (159), the beleaguered eccentric at odds with the world and stubbornly doing his own thing. As he says in the just-quoted letter to Mrs. Watson, "it's that what I'm trying to do,or rather who I'd like to be(the only value which,for me,makes my living worth while)quite incidentally but inexorably unmakes most 'values'; rendering them less than valueless." He feels his paintings have received little recognition (228), that he has fought a twenty-year battle against liberalism and socialism (228), that he opposes the book distributing and reviewing marketplace (243), that he deliberately insults "the powersthatseem" (245), that the poet cannot "give a hangnail for social respectability" (256), and that he must refuse an invitation to the White House

(275). He must uncompromisingly man his personal barricades: he hates the radio (174–75, 195), the critics (237, 252), and the *New Yorker* (230, 245); and he refuses to teach (167, 202, 222, 257) or hold any regular job, to appear on symposia or give autographs; and he disparages automobiles and movies. After years of such energy-consuming battles, it is no wonder that he feels that New York City has deteriorated and turns, as we shall see, to the solace of simple, bucolic virtues.

Indeed, the really significant point is the effect such a life experience and its accompanying defenses had upon the inner structure of his emotional life. Certainly, we know from the published *oeuvre* that Cummings could be a hater, but what we get a less clear picture of there is the pain, depression, and self-doubt that inevitably must underlie such hostility. The problem in the published writings, as we have seen, is not that he is so naive as to lack a sane and realistic sense of the evil in the world — his innocence needn't be protected against *that* charge. The problem is that he sometimes lacks a sense of any *relation* to that evil, either as it might impinge upon him and get him down, or as it might find a reflection within himself. His desired stance, as I have suggested, is to proclaim he is above being affected by it and is indeed separate from it.

But doubts and black moods are precisely what he could not keep out of his letters.[2] Speaking to his mother about his first wife's desertion, he says, "am sitting on a large piece of almost nothing taking my own photograph with a shutterless camera" (108). Many years later, he writes to the daughter whom that ex-wife kept from him and hopes he has had some influence upon her life: "Being myself nearly sans time-sense(except as rhythm)I can only guess when certain still-vivid childhood experiences may have occurred. But shall never forget how my staunch(then as now)friend Sibley Watson,by way of comforting our unhappy nonhero,gently reminded him that the greatly(to me)wise Freud says a child's self('psyche')is already formed at whatever age you were when we lost each other" (269).

In 1948 he writes to a friend, "it's good to hear that you've outgrown your 'great depressions.' I've the very great honour to inform you that you're way ahead of me! Am possibly emerging from an impossible & v.v. [vice versa] one at the so-called present writing" (186). He writes to MacLeish about being depressed over his arthritis (189), and to another that he reads Santayana "when an UNworld threatens to get me down" (262). And he has moments of profound self-doubt: "why doesn't he do this,do that [he imagines people asking]?why,when he has such&such a talent & could surely score a success there or here,does he renege & refuse; balk,stall,backtrack;hide from,dodge,or even insult those who'd like to help him;put absurd obstacles in his own way,& otherwise play the neurotic to perfection? . . . Am I wrong about myself? Does my picture of me fail as a likeness?" (188). Or again: "why does little Estlin find it so hard to understand that everything almost(& almost everybody)'s perpetually disintegrating;[as well as re-?" (203). And again: "Tell me now,Hildegarde [it is significant that each of these moments is confided to the Watsons],what do you think:am I suffering from what 'the liberals' entitle 'failure of nerve,'or from something else most beautifully described by Quintus H[oratius Flaccus = 'Horace'] as 'nec pietas moram';or may my unending timidities harbour a diminutive amount of truth?" (212).

We also know from the published *oeuvre* that Cummings was a transcender, but what is also less specific there, in consequence of what we've been noticing so far, is *what* and *how* he transcends, as well as what it means specifically to him as a person. Counterbalancing the hate, pain, depression, and self-doubt are strong moments in the letters—not merely of acceptance of suffering—but rather of intense self-awareness and inner integration. Here he goes behind his own defensive stance and risks facing the void: I myself am Hell. Writing to his mother in 1941 about their being 101% New Englanders, he remarks that Gilbert Seldes accused him once "of what he called 'the egocentric predicament.' If Gilbert had been a Catholic he'd have used another phrase—'the sin of pride.' For what he meant was that really,underneath everything,I considered myself pretty dam [sic] omniscient.—Well,ourhero(being a New Englander)vigorously denied all. But very gradually I began to notice that if something happened which prevented me from doing as I pleased,then(by Jove)I tended to feel downright frustrated:nay, even personally insulted! Talk about "childish"! Maybe,some day,I'll be blessed with a touch of true humility" (159).

Writing to Pound in 1947, he said, "But more & more,as I grow,is the antediluvian undersigned delighted by Doctor Jung's terrafirma riposte when a desperate wouldbe dogooder demanded what can be done to make better the world?quote Jung,make thyself better" (176). He writes to his sister in 1954, "But feel I'm somehow gradually evolving;despite selfpity narcissism an inferiority complex & possibly several other psychic ailments" (238). In 1955 he writes to Mrs. Watson, "must confess I attribute my physical ills to socalled nervous tension" (245). In explicating "Hello is what a mirror says" (*1 x 1*, #XXX) for an inquiring reader, he says: "*true wars are never won*;since they are inward,not outward,and necessitate facing one's self" (247).

The sense that hatred is often a projection outward of what one hates in oneself is also clearly realized several times in the letters. In 1946 he writes, "(may I quote Confucius?) 'gentleman blames himself,ungentleman blames others'" (170). Writing to a French friend in 1949, he says, "if only we can transcend the hate which makes us willy-nilly become what we most detest,& somehow achieve the capacity to love . . . then our Selves will survive:no harm can touch Them" (195). He writes to Pound in 1955, "if am not most grossly mistaken,'twas David called Thoreau observed he had never met—or hoped to meet—a man worse than himself / talents differ:if heroical thine be cursing swine & ringing nex,our tolerant unhero may only re-mark(vide 6 nonlectures page 70)that 'hatred bounces'" (243). The reference would seem to be to Cummings' 1945 contribution to Oscar Williams' anthology called *The War Poets*, which he included in *i:SIX NONLECTURES*: "fear and hate the liar . . . where he should be feared and hated:in yourselves." There is also reference there to Cummings' favorite Bible passage, John, viii, 7, "this masterpoem of human perception, whose seventh verse alone exterminates all conventional morality—'He that is without sin among you, let him first cast a stone at her'" (*i:SIX NONLECTURES*, 66–67).

V

Well then: Fine&Dandy, as Cummings himself might say. But what puzzles is how all this compares with his own characteristic you-and-me-against-the-world stance, and in particular the many virulent satires where he does more than his own share of "cursing swine & ringing nex," as if he might indeed be without sin and thus free to cast his stone. Then again, I suppose it is not so puzzling after all, for the kind of integration Cummings reached, and under the conditions of his own particular life experience, is extremely rare and difficult to achieve, let alone sustain, and mood swings and ambivalence are inevitably to be expected—as the complicated contexts of many of the above quotes in the letters amply illustrate.

A similar split is to be found in the structure of his intellectual life as well. His antagonism to science is, of course, well known, and it finds some characteristic expression here in the letters (85, 130, 265). But there is also, surprisingly, an admission of respect for science, and this is not quite so well-known. Working on a poem, which was apparently never published, about the waning moon descending the afternoon sky, he asks his sister in 1956 "whether or not an astronomer would accept this image of mine. . . . If not,shall have to change my poem in deference to science" (253–53). Even more important, as we've previously noted, is his appreciation of Yeats' "equal understanding of perfectly opposed viewpoints—collective & individual,systematic & spontaneous,rational & instinctive" (255).

One could wish that his attitudes toward politics were as clearly integrated.[3] Most characteristically, both in the letters and published writings, his stance is determinedly apolitical, as befits an artist whose vision is transcendental. Politics, after all, deals with the conflicts and polarizations of the material and societal world, whose values are oriented around power and success—everything Cummings realizes he opposes. He rejects joiners, reformers, do-gooders, gangs, the tyranny of the majority, socialism, communism, fascism, and liberalism (145, 150, 162, 173, 176, 225, 228, 250, 254). And yet he sympathized with the victims of the May Day fiasco in 1919 (60), excitedly followed the political news from Russia in 1920 (69), called himself a Leninite or Trotskyite (72), and claimed in 1923 that he admired Russia (104). Of course, this was when he was still a fairly young man.

But what happened later was still less apolitical. Writing to his daughter in 1951, he recounts the following puzzling anecdote: "And as for surprise:perhaps the only equally-surprised humanbeing is,or was,my little newyorker pal Morrie Werner;when he demanded pointblank why I called myself 'a good Republican,'& I instantly answered 'because the Republicans have an elephant.' Morrie looked at our unhero as if Morrie's head would come off;then he moaned that I was kidding him,'no' I said 'I mean it':then he almost fainted from shock(but what better reason could anybody have?) After some terrible moments,Morrie's weak faint trembling voice asked dazedly 'but don't you like donkeys?' 'Yes' I admitted frankly 'but not so well as elephants.' There was a frightening pause. Then he slowly whispered 'je-sus-chr-ist'" (214).

Cummings, of course, had early and late a fetish for elephants, but what his Republicanism means became clearer when we took up *Adventures in Value* in chapter 2. Here it may help to quote from a letter to his sister in 1953: "With every serious anarchist who ever lived,I assume that 'all governments are founded on force'" (223). He opposes, of course, Big Govern-

ment, but he also opposes Big Business and the Pentagon: his Republicanism was of a rather special kind—a form, as I have said, of the agrarian,
New England self-reliance philosophy, where the independent farmer dis-
trusts the politicians over there in the state house or down there in Washington. His own explanation couldn't be clearer in its delightedly frank ir-
rationality, but he was not really a farmer, after all, nor did he escape that
confusion of categories I spoke of in chapter 7 which can occur when a
transcender becomes a social critic without shifting gears.

11

Knowing and Remembering Cummings

Interestingly enough, this chapter is based on Cummings' letters to me, and, because they are written from the position of master to disciple, they contain very little of that inner turmoil we've been noticing up to now. Indeed, because that disciple was so entirely respectful of the master's inner privacy, he positively *avoided* any probing into that area while Cummings was still alive and for years afterwards. First written as a talk in 1979 to be given at Temple University by invitation of Richard Kennedy, this chapter was originally published in the *Harvard Library Bulletin* in 1981 and is taken up primarily with showing the poet's concerned responsiveness to me and my interest in his writings. Its unalloyed tone of respect will provide a respite from the more complex attitudes expressed in the surrounding chapters.

I

To talk about my relationship with E. E. Cummings is, for better or worse, also to talk about my own life, for, as I go over my connection with him and his work, I find that it has played—and still plays—a large and significant part in what I have no other choice but to call my self. I shall try, however, to stand to one side and put my focus where it belongs, on Cummings himself. Still, the fact remains that a specific phase of the lives and careers of both Cummings and myself unfolded and concluded during our relationship, and that this relationship had a determinative effect on what shape that phase of my life took, as well as some small but perceptible effect on his.

The story of this relationship coincides with the story, first and foremost, of the rise of his career as a poet, and at the same time, alas, of his aging and death as a man. It is also, secondarily, the story of the beginning and development of my career as an academic. And it is, in the third place, as I have suggested, the story of the interconnections between these two narratives. Since much of my career as an academic, as well as much of my personal life, was based on my work on Cummings, it is clear that his effect on me has been deep and powerful. While I make no claim regarding my effect on the development of either Cummings' art or life, for it is obvious that both would have progressed pretty much the same without me, I do believe that I have contributed—along with many others—to the growth of his reception. In several instances, in fact, as we shall see, I gratefully played a direct part in promoting and guiding his public appearances. Nevertheless, my main emphasis here will be on how he seemed to me, how he acted toward me, and on his generosity to me, which I experienced all over again as I read through my file of his letters in preparation for this talk.

My relationship with Cummings, as it emerges from our correspondence, falls into three roughly equal chronological periods, plus a prologue and epilogue. These periods—and I am very interested in this phenomenon, for the pattern cannot be entirely accidental—are marked by crucial turns in the careers of each of us at around the same times. The prologue has to do with my beginning to know him through reading his books. The first main period starts with my Harvard honors thesis on his poetry and ends as I am going to the University of Connecticut and he is coming to Cambridge. The second and third begin with his Charles Eliot Norton Lectures at Harvard, go on to involve the planning and writing of my first book on Cummings, and end when it is finally published. And the epilogue concerns the writing of my second book on Cummings, my visit to Silver Lake, his death, and my family's move to New York.

II

I began turning consistently to poetry when I was a high school student in Brooklyn during the early 1940s. I remember being moved by Whitman and Browning, and wondering if I could ever come to absorb other poets—such as Keats and Shelley—whose books I saw on bookstore and library shelves. I tried to write poems of my own. But most of all, I discovered E. E. Cummings and felt I had found someone who seemed to be talking from within myself, telling me things I was feeling but had not yet learned to express: that to love was the purpose of life, that to be oneself was the struggle of life, and that what others did and said was not necessarily better or more true. And he said these things with such a joy, freshness, and verve that they felt irresistible. He seemed to take pleasure in writing poems and in communicating his excitement directly to the reader.

True, he was an experimenter, a rebel, an iconoclast, and he was not content either with the commonplace and ordinary or with commonplace and ordinary ways of writing. Yet he seemed creative rather than destructive, serious rather than arbitrary, and he repaid close attention. If he rejected the commonplace and ordinary, it was because he was reaching for the basic and the universal. If he appealed to an adolescent's need for rebellion, he also appealed to his need for self-definition; if he spoke to this adolescent's sense of dissatisfaction with his environment, he also promoted his need to grow. This, I find, is what those critics who complain about Cummings' "immaturity" have been missing: that if there is "adolescence" in Cummings, it is not a symbol simply of rebellion but rather of the life-long imperative to grow, which does not end with adolescence.

My closest friends in high school were also interested in Cummings—as was Zelda, my wife-to-be—and we would read his poems to each other after school. We had *The Enormous Room* (1922) in the Modern Library edition (1934), *Him* of 1927, *Eimi* of 1933, and the 1938 *Collected Poems. 50 Poems* of 1940 was still a new book, and *1 x 1* of 1944 seemed to have been written especially for us. In those days, the Eighth Street bookstores in Manhattan were serious shops devoted to the arts, and I spent many an afternoon poking about those dusty interiors looking for Cummingsiana, somehow conscious that he himself, who lived nearby, might be strolling in Washington Square just down the street.

By 1943 and 1944 my friends and I were barely eighteen or nineteen and were in the service. I carried my Cummings with me, and not simply in my heart, when I went into the Navy V-12 college training program—a wartime expedient, designed to accelerate the supply of commissioned officers to the fleet—as an engineering student at M.I.T. and then at Harvard, and subsequently served on a destroyer in the Atlantic Fleet, for it seemed to me that I had especial need of him then.

Zelda and I were married in 1945, and by 1946 I had returned to Harvard on the GI bill as an English major. I went out for honors, and I had as additional requirements to take Latin, special tutorials, written and oral comps, and do a thesis. I naturally chose to write my thesis on Cummings and asked the late Theodore Spencer if he would serve as my advisor. He was delighted, telling me he was a friend of Cummings, and kindly suggested that I write to him. I did write around February or March of 1947, and this began our fifteen-year relationship.

So ends this prologue—except that Michael, my son, who shall figure in this narrative more than once, was born around that same time—in April 1947. And it might be worth saying something briefly about what Cummings' life was like just before I met him. After many years of separation, he and his daughter Nancy had recently rediscovered one another, and also he had lost his mother early in 1947. He was fifty-three at this time, and he was, as his published letters to others reveal (see chapter 10), going through a certain amount of inner struggle and self-questioning. He was, in addition, facing the coming fulfillment of his career. I was twenty-two and facing five more years of Harvard and ten or so at the University of Connecticut.

III

My letter of self-introduction, telling him about my thesis plans and asking if he would answer certain questions, brought a rapid—if brief—reply by postcard: "Fire away," he wrote bravely, not suspecting what he was getting himself into. Unfortunately, because I did not start keeping copies of my letters to him until seven years later, it is difficult for me to recall exactly what I asked him in my next letter.[1] One can infer, however, that it must have been a request for clarification of his values, for his subsequent reply represents an attempt at such clarification. In this letter, which is in the published *Selected Letters* (174–5), he tries to explain himself to an unknown young man writing an honors thesis on his poetry, and he does so by talking about his apartment and a neighbor who listens to the radio all the time. Although I really did not understand this explanation until some years later, I was awed to receive this carefully composed and carefully typed letter of one-and-a-half single-spaced pages from such a man: it was just like him, just like his published writings, idiosyncratic typographical touches and all, and yet at the same time it was personal, courteous, and considerate.

Whatever inner problems he may have been experiencing, he put them to one side as he pondered what to say to this student from nowhere. Indeed, as I look over my file of correspondence from him—he also would write to Zelda on occasion, and later his wife, Marion, would write too—a file which includes just over 140 communications, I find that he was always unfailingly and consistently warm, concerned, encouraging, and supportive in relation to me and my family.

I was scheduled for mid-year graduation, and sometime in the fall of 1947 I completed my thesis and sent him a copy. He was very pleased, even touched, by this immature, if wholehearted, early critical effort of mine: "thanks many times for sending me your essay! Reading it has cheered,& cheers,&(no doubt)will cheer,me deeply. . . . possibly the letter which you wrote & sent with the essay is an even greater compliment than the essay itself. . . . permit me to thank you for this letter,& to assure you I appreciate(in my own proud & humble way)its true affection[.]" And then he invited me to come and visit him and Marion, who would have "the pleasure & the honour," as he put it, "of providing a touch of tea or a whisper of whitehorse or both." And so, armed, as I recall, with a folder of pictures of my infant son taken at three months of age, I boarded the train from Boston to New York for my first sight in the flesh of my hero—or "nonhero," as he preferred—on a Sunday afternoon, 23 November, as it happened.

Cummings was a man of medium height, slender, and almost bald, dressed in casual clothing, and he was in the habit of tilting his straight-backed chair against the rear wall, hooking his hands behind his head, and keeping up a joyous, amused, and witty stream of talk. In the meantime, Marion, also dressed casually, would busy herself at her tea table by the front window, and would enter the conversation at her own pace.

I subsequently wrote to him about passing my honors orals, and his reply, recalling his own similar experience, is also printed in *Selected Letters* (181). By now it was early 1948, I had graduated, submitted my essay for the Bowdoin Prize for my honors thesis, and was taking my first graduate courses. One of these was in American literature with Howard Mumford Jones, and when this eminent professor made some less-than-enthusiastic remarks about Cummings in one of his lectures, I respectfully but determinedly approached him after class and suggested that perhaps there was more to be said on the subject. The good professor took kindly to my temerity and wondered if I would present a lecture to the class on Cummings. I picked up the gauntlet and did just that—my first experience in front of a class. It went well enough, and Professor Jones asked me to be one of his assistants for the following year, a connection which gave me my start up the academic ladder and for which I am everlastingly grateful. When I wrote to Cummings about the whole affair, he replied: "am naturally delighted(& flattered)to learn of your battle in behalf of someone who shall be nameless. Thanks! / & thank you especially for reading the poems sans microphone. That's a mighty compliment,& I mightily appreciate it[.]"

The next winter Zelda and I attended a performance of *Him* at the Provincetown Playhouse on MacDougal Street, and I wrote to Cummings about it and also about having won a Bowdoin Prize and election to Phi Beta Kappa the previous spring. He wrote that he was not too happy about that particular production, and that he was "a trifle jealous" of me. "Picture me, year after Harvard year," he wrote in early 1949, "vainly attempting to win something;even(in an effort to attain ΦBK, & thereby please my good parents)declaiming at perhaps Commencement." But he congratulated me on my assistantship and concluded, "I have known 3 or 4 teachers in all my life(they are born). The rest is racket. And here's wishing you are born." I seem to have expressed doubts, however, for he wrote in March of that year to encourage me: "my advice(perhaps disagreeably simple)is,thank God that in this loveless unday you've human beings who love you & whom you love;do,as nearly as ever you may,what you feel is natural for you to do:& waste as little light as possible worrying over what you might or should or shouldn't or mightn't have done or do or be doing. Above all & under,don't be afraid—e.g. of making mistakes;& remember it's more than likely they'll make yourself[.]"

During some of those summers, when I was not registered for courses, I would attempt to supplement my inadequate income by day and to study in the evenings. One of those supplemental attempts was door-to-door selling—first pots, pans, and steam irons, and then sets of *The Book of Knowledge*. Cummings' response, as usual, throws an interesting light on himself. Sending greetings to me as "The Industrial Hero," he wrote, "don't know whether I should congratulate you more vividly on (A) your inability to sell

1 pot or pan in 6 working days, or (Z) your ability to clear 90$ in 7 days by any means whatsoever e.g. selling encyclopedias." (I interpolate here that I was scarcely able to average half that amount over the long haul.) "But let me confess that once," Cummings continued, "when the undersigned was (broke)n,he found myself on the verge of peddling Current Opinion from-door-to-door—whereat I suffered a sort of faintingfit de luxe;& was sent right home(sans le sou)per the kindly Yale man who'd given me my proverbial chance."

In the fall of 1949, he gave a reading at Brandeis, and we saw him there. Sometime shortly after, he came by our Cambridge "veterans'" apartment in Andover Court—not far from his boyhood home on 104 Irving Street—for a brief visit, when our son was around two-and-a-half years old. I was not home, as it happened, and he came upon Zelda and Michael. She invited him in and told the child that this was E. E. Cummings. Michael looked up at him and without pause said, "Then why doesn't he say 'now i love you and you love me, and books are shuter than books can be'?" (1 x 1, #LIV). Cummings then, with pause, and an aside to Zelda describing butterflies in his chest, identified himself obligingly in Michael's terms by reciting the lines in question.

By 1950 Cummings' career was beginning perceptibly to rise. *Xaipe* appeared, and he was at last beginning to win prestigious grants and prizes, be asked more frequently to give readings, and be able to travel more often abroad. Around that same time, I was finishing up my graduate course work and was starting to focus on the problem of choosing a topic for my doctoral dissertation. As I consulted with the then-chairman of the English department, he made it clear to me that the thesis should not be done on someone who was still living because, for better or worse, publication and job opportunities should be greater if I became a specialist on someone earlier and therefore safer.

I notice now with a certain grim satisfaction that Cummings was to write me sometime after, "The only trouble with you(ofcourse)is that I am not 'Tears Eliot." The fact that academia has since changed with regard to the kind of attention it pays not only to contemporary writers in general but also to Cummings in particular can only be salutary. Nevertheless, I did not feel free enough within myself at that time to take my stand at the outposts, and I must have written something to that effect to Cummings, for I find him saying in the late summer of that year: "but such considerations become as lessthannothing compared with something which matters truly:je veux dire that if ever a time existed when every writer worthhissalt should 'think of books & poems I want to write,'it's everlastingly Now[.]"

During our last year in Cambridge, 1951–52, we were able finally to move to Harvard's more permanent apartments in Holden Green, the antisemitism debate appeared in the *Congress Weekly*,[2] and plans were afoot to have him come to Cambridge as the Charles Eliot Norton Lecturer for the following year. On the antisemitism debate, Cummings wrote to me as follows: "as nearly as our nonhero can make out,any gangster's chief characteristic is hisorher total lack of a(strictly divine)sense of humor. Consider supersubmorons-in-question. Were the proverbial shoe in the other foot,they'd all be howling FreedomOfSpeech like—as my friend David Diamond says—crazy." I had written a letter to the editor in defense of Cummings, but the *Congress Weekly* decided not to print it. I then wrote an article on the question, and it was published in *The Reconstructionist*.[3] When I sent a copy to Cummings, he replied, "every so seldom,our unhero feels even exceptionally minus;whereupon(& this is a Mystery)out of all nowhere comes some amazing friendliness."

In the meantime, negotiations were proceeding apace for the Norton appointment. Professor John H. Finley, Jr., under whom I was serving as a teaching fellow in the humanities, was apparently in charge of the Harvard side of it, and, learning of my connection with the poet, he asked me whether I thought Cummings would accept the invitation, what would attract him, and whether I would write to him about it. In April of 1952 Cummings wrote to me as follows: "if your 'erstwhile boss' hadn't written as he did,our nonhero would never have 'accepted.' Even with such marvellous encouragement I spent several difficult weeks deciding. . . . now let me frankly crave friendly advice:what sort of 'lectures' should the ignorant undersigned attempt? 'Criticism'& 'scholarship' are out:I wouldn't(possibly since am neither 'scholar' nor 'critic')like either if either were good. What remains?to give readings of my own work(prose,plays,poems)? Every suggestion gratefully received & cherished strictly sub-sub-rosa[.]"

I wrote back saying that in my opinion what his Harvard audience would like to hear would be some account of himself, his career, and his stance as a writer—interwoven, if he chose, with readings from his own works. He worked on his "nonlectures" over the summer and wrote me in September that my suggestions helped. Later he wrote, "have been congratulated on your idea(for 1st-3-nonlectures)& at least once gave credit where 'tis due;perhaps always." And later, when I wrote to say how good we thought the nonlectures were and how much we enjoyed them, he replied: "Praise from the(softly speaking)instigator of directly half & indirectly all my non-lectures is more than praise,& am naturally more than grateful. Occasion-ally—I must admit—our egocentric nonhero wishes he could believe in quite-unselfishly doing-good-unto-others;perhaps one merciful day he will. But,even now,said hamstrung hedonist can & does rejoice in his benefactor's however generous pleasure[.]" As we shall see, however, in this instigator's opinion, he was not so hamstrung as he feared.

IV

But I find I have gotten slightly ahead of my story. Having completed my doctorate in the spring of 1952, I (and my family) left Cambridge for my first full-time teaching position, at the University of Connecticut in Storrs. It is ironic that we left even as the Cummingses were arriving, but it does help to point up that strange pattern formed by the intersection of our lives which I have already commented upon. The distance between Storrs and Cambridge is not great, however, and we did manage to attend most or all of the six nonlectures. The main business of this next period, which ex-tends until 1956, was getting established at UConn, having a daughter, Janet, and beginning my first book on Cummings. Regarding this latter, Cummings was, as always, unstintingly helpful and encouraging; and Marion, who was assuming the role of his archivist, began writing to us as well. Also, I gradu-ally began to see the value of keeping copies of my own letters, especially in connection with this project.

Having learned of my intention to write a book about him, Cummings wrote me in the spring of 1954 and offered to help: "Marion,who salvaged my mother's scrapbook of clippings when 104 Irving street changed masters & who's long been collecting reviews etc on her devoted own & who now possesses an extensive group of mags comprising my graphic efforts,will gladly open said archives for your illustrious inspection. Biography,however,is something else. Very frankly:I feel that my life is my work(paintings &drawings times poetry & prose)—a stance impossible for any 'publicity'-crazed unworld to partially semiappreciate;but which am confident you'll easily more than understand[.]" One can readily sympa-thize with these feelings, and one recalls the many other authors who have expressed similar sentiments. A writer exposes a lot of himself to the public through his writings, but he does this by choice, wanting the rest of himself to remain private. Or, at least, he does not want to give himself away—and preferably only to careful hands—without a struggle. Cummings was shortly to do so in relation to Charles Norman—and also, as we shall see, although I had no desire to do a biography, to me.

Our daughter was born in June, and I include a letter from Marion in July simply to show her generosity: "Congratulations and good wishes!!! We should have acknowledged the arrival of the miracle before this but I've been away—illness in my family—and when I'm away things pile up, letters get lost and very important announcements get misplaced. / As I'm sure Janet has everything she needs, please, Zelda, buy yourself something giddy, or austere, whichever you wish."[4] A check was enclosed. In October, *Poems 1923–1954* was published by Harcourt, and Marion wrote me as follows: "Re the new POEMS have you see[n] Mr. Jarrell's Sunday Times revue? And do you know why he should do such a thing? I take it he is moved by great personal animus to Cummings and wonder why." I had written a letter to the editor protesting that condescending review of over thirty years of work by one of our major poets, and it appeared, along with several others, in *NYTBR*, December 5, 1954. Cummings did, however, receive a special citation from the National Book Awards in the following year for that collection.

The pace of our correspondence quickens considerably during these years of the preparation and publication of my book. In the spring of 1955 I asked him if he would answer questions and whether I could be permitted to examine any of his manuscripts. He said he would "cheerfully attempt elucidation," and the remainder of this letter, giving me permission to see some manuscripts on condition that I keep them to myself, appears in *Selected Letters* (245). I thereupon asked for clarifications in over thirty poems I had trouble with, and he replied, repeating his condition about the manuscripts—which turned out to be the "rosetree" variants—and enclosing almost four single-spaced typed pages of elucidations.

At this time, I was hoping that my work would do something to make it harder for hostile critics to repeat the same old negative clichés about Cummings' poetry, and Marion, who had been arranging for me to examine the scrapbooks and manuscripts, wrote to me that she sometimes got "so depressed to realize that so much of his work is dismissed as a joke, amusing but not really funny like O. Nash. I remember Miriam Patchen expressing amazement when I told her that we couldn't go to her house because Cummings was working on the Krazy Kat introduction[5] and couldn't stop. She said, 'But he was working on that last month!' I, '—Well, he still is—he's on his 19th draft,'—She 'Really! Why Kenneth just writes things right off and never changes a word.'" Marion then wrote that the "rosetree" variants had been "worked on over a period of more than ten years."

In November I received a telegram from both of them congratulating me on my first chapter, a copy of which I had sent shortly before. Beginning early in 1956 Cummings went over my manuscript chapter by chapter, sending me corrections, suggestions, and appreciations. I was also asking if he would give me permission to quote from the variants, and he was beginning to weaken. Since the manuscript sheets did not come in their order of composition, I was trying to find a way of analyzing the growth of the poem. Cummings gave me permission to write an analysis of the variants, but still on condition that I not quote directly from them. He was also trying to help me find a publisher for the book. Finally, I asked permission to put a photographic copy of one of the "rosetree" sheets in my book, and he agreed. The matter was settled, and I was able to quote from the manuscript extensively. When I sent them the results, he replied, "Which of us was more amazed by chapter five,no se;but do know that I—who never touch detectivestories—told Marion,who's an authority thereon,that your analysis of the 'rosetree' manuscript struck me as positively 'eerie':& she whisperingly agreed."

V

That was in November of 1956, and negotiations were underway at the same time for Cummings to give a reading at UConn the following spring as the main feature of our projected fine arts festival. The next phase of our story, then, begins here and ends in 1960 with the publication of my book. These are the years, also, of his appearance at the Boston Fine Arts Festival and his receipt of the Bollingen Award (both 1957), and the appearance of 95 Poems (1958) and A Miscellany—the latter compiled by Cummings' editor and literary agent, George Firmage, whose book-length bibliography appeared in 1960—as well as of Charles Norman's biography, The Magic-Maker, in 1958.

Although John Malcolm Brinnin, who was also at UConn at the time, would have been the obvious choice to serve as Cummings' impresario for the spring visit, I gratefully accepted the offer to perform that service.

Cummings was delighted, and we began making arrangements for his trip, his schedule, his room, and so on. I also elicited a poem from him to be published in the *Fine Arts Festival Magazine*. In April Zelda and I went to New York to discuss last-minute arrangements with Cummings, and shortly thereafter the event actually occurred.

✳   ✳   ✳

I went to Bradley Field, just north of Hartford, to await his approach, but his plane was delayed because of bad weather in New York. He finally arrived, somewhat fatigued—he had also been ill shortly before—and I drove him to our campus apartment in Storrs (somewhat grander than the one in Cambridge he had been welcomed to some seven years before, but still a bit snug). We had dinner for him and several of our friends, and then he went upstairs to rest on a board he had to carry for his arthritic back. Later, at his reading, we had a wonderful crowd, and I spoke in my introduction of my true feeling for him, and he was quite moved. His reading itself was, as usual, a carefully prepared and beautiful performance, and he met with students afterwards. Then, after a modest faculty reception, I brought him, no doubt exhausted, to the room we had reserved for him at a local inn. John Brinnin drove him back to the airport the next morning.

Shortly thereafter I wrote him about how well the occasion had gone, and he replied by thanking us—and also John—for our assistance, and concluding: "am glad-&-thankful the students more than survived their shakeup. Bully(as Teddy R would exclaim)for them! When I asked a member of the 'younger' generation how he & his friends felt concerning one of my nonlectures at Sanders Theatre,he replied(smiling agreeably) 'for us it was like being hit over the head with a baseballbat[.]'" But if he could hit like a bat, it was surely with a gentle touch. I have recorded in my second book, *The Growth of a Writer* (1964), an incident which occurred following his Storrs reading and which does much to bring out the measure of the man: "So that people would not confuse him with Elvis Presley, as he said, he refused to give autographs. This was not mere crankiness, however: . . . when one of my students—a charming young lady—seemed disappointed at being refused an autograph, he gallantly and wittily redeemed the situation by impulsively seizing her hand and kissing it. I am sure this meant more to her than his signature!" (174).

And I finally have come to understand the meaning of what he said in his first letter to me about that neighbor whose radio bothered him, when he concluded, "all this—the 2 perfectly different tastes,the 3 floors,the old house—is a metaphor,a parable, . . ." for I see now with the intensest clarity the following phrase: "the last thing I'd like to do is to hurt the little man." This artist, whom critics have accused of being a perpetual adolescent and a snob, was almost more concerned with the feelings of others than he was about being himself. If he did not want to become a public plaything, he nevertheless would give without let or hindrance to anyone who took the trouble to regard him as a human being.

In the meantime, a chapter of my book was being published in *PMLA*, and another, with Cummings' help, in *The Literary Review*,[6] but the book itself was still looking for a home. Several other matters also occupied our correspondence. In April of 1958 Cummings had gone with Marion to visit Ezra Pound at St. Elizabeth's Hospital in Washington, D.C., and he wrote us a postcard in which he quoted her reactions: "'I wish' she murmured 'that the people who say Ezra's not mad could have seen him as we did today.'" Pound, of course, had been there for twelve years by then. Cummings wrote again in June: "re EP's cantos:have never shared the enthusiasm of their interpreters;possibly because I've a notion he abuses 'and' worse than anyone since WWhitman."

By the following year I had written a Postscript on 95 *Poems* for my book, and I was discussing revisions with the Johns Hopkins University Press, which was to accept the manuscript that fall. Our correspondence during the fall and winter was primarily concerned with the various problems of securing a photograph of him for the book jacket, deciding on the final text of his poems, proofreading them, and so on. *E. E. Cummings: The Art of His Poetry* appeared in the spring of 1960, and Cummings wrote in June that he "wouldn't have anybody else 'the author of the first book of criticism' on my poetry. (Owing to said first book,found myself slighting all my chores;& was compelled to punish me by going without you for at least a month[.])"

VI

The epilogue, which covers the final period of our relationship from 1960 to 1962, finds me beginning my second book on Cummings for the Southern Illinois University Press. Naturally, I had not planned to write that book, if at all, for some time, but Harry T. Moore had written to me requesting that I do it for their "Cross-currents: Modern Critiques Series," and naturally, I could not refuse. Certainly, I wanted to focus on the prose works, as well as to treat the poetry in a somewhat different way, and again Cummings was agreeable to helping me. I remember especially his comments on *Him* and *Tom*. He wrote me in July of 1962 about *Tom* as follows: "LKirstein commissioned me to write a ballet-scenario:I asked Marion what its subject should be,& she suggested Uncle Tom's Cabin:I wrote the scenario, for which David Diamond made a complete orchestral score,but Balanchine balked: . . . when Marion made her suggestion,I'd never taken seriously UT'sC or read it carefully all through;though well aware that President ALincoln,meeting the authoress thereof,observed 'so you're the little lady who made this terrible war.' I now red[*sic*]—& was astonished. My scenario is the direct result of this astonishment[.]"

Meanwhile, I had published an essay on Cummings and modernism in *Forum* (chapter 1, above), and he responded, with his usual generosity, by saying, "that 'Forum' essay is what my beloved Uncle George would call a corkerino/felicitations!" I was also working on an analysis of the Cummings criticism from the beginning to the early 1960s, to be given as a talk at the MLA convention in Washington at the end of 1962 (chapter 6, above). Our last connections with Cummings on this earth were a trip to Silver Lake and a few postcards he sent just before his death.

During the second week of August we finally had worked up enough courage—and faith in our old automobile—to hazard the journey to New Hampshire in acceptance of the Cummingses' many hospitable invitations, and they arranged to put us up overnight at their Joy Farm house. I recall discussing with them the proofs of their soon-to-be published book of Marion's photographs and Cummings' captions, called *Adventures in Value* (Harcourt, 1962), and the manuscript of Cummings' latest collection of poems, which was issued posthumously as *73 Poems* (1963). I also recall with great pleasure that Marion was much taken with our lovely daughter Janet, who was eight at the time, and said she would like to photograph her some day.

A few weeks after our return to Connecticut, we received a terrible call from Marion telling us that Cummings had died, saying the funeral would be a small private affair, and asking me to phone some others in turn. Having just seen him so recently, I felt this news with especial force. I looked back now at our visit with wonder at how fleetingly it had passed, how he had taken us for a walk on top of the house, shown us a drawing of an elephant he had done as a child, given our children a wooden letterbox with "Joy Farm" engraved on it with a wood-burning tool. . . .

The following year we packed up and moved to New York, bringing to a close this part of my life and career, and returning to where I had begun for a new beginning. My second book on Cummings was published in the spring of 1964, and during these years we received a number of letters from Marion, who continued to help me with my Cummings work. In June of 1969 we sadly received a printed invitation to a memorial service for Marion Morehouse Cummings, to be held at the Jefferson Market Library on Sixth Avenue, just a stone's throw from their apartment in Patchin Place. Zelda and I attended, and we recall Robert Lowell, as the featured speaker, talking of Marion and Cummings and reading some of Cummings' poetry. We also recall the wizened presence of Ezra Pound, and I think now of Marion's comment about him eleven years previously when she and Cummings had visited him at St. Elizabeth's. Pound has since died also, and so, alas, has Lowell—as well as Jarrell. Our sense of uncompleted mourning found closure in that small hushed assemblage as the relationship between Marion and Cummings was celebrated through the reading of his love poems to her.

12

"so many selves"

:On Kennedy's *Dreams in the Mirror*

Originally published in 1984 as the concluding section of "Further Developments," chapter 9 above, this material is placed here because it contains my attempts to understand more fully the writer as a person and the relationship between that person and the writer.[1]

I

I cannot convey what a profoundly moving effect Kennedy's *Dreams in the Mirror* (1980) has had and no doubt will continue to have on me. And I don't mean merely by way of nostalgia—I mean by way of revealing Cummings to me in many new lights. However this may be, it will no doubt remain the definitive biography for the foreseeable future. Written in the objective mode, it is based on a rich mine of firsthand material—interviews, travels, documents, letters, papers, manuscripts, notebooks, and so on—it gains rather than suffers from Kennedy's never having known Cummings personally, and it is not likely to be easily superseded in our time.

Dreams in the Mirror contains thirty-two information-filled but lucid chapters. Although it is not bound to any single overriding theme or thesis, and although it is not prone to any excessively psychological speculation, it does seem to be primarily concerned, according to the first, introductory, chapter, with the problem of the multiplicity of Cummings' selves, and the mystery of his secret or private self. The latter self Kennedy sees as embodied in the lower-case "i," as "corresponding to such characters as Pierrot, Petrouchka, and Charlie Chaplin's role of the little tramp." This self is revealed most clearly, says Kennedy, in "anyone lived in a pretty how town" (50 *Poems*, #29), and then he comments: "How far away from all this seems the general career of E. E. Cummings, the public figure who was one of the leaders of the literary revolt of the 1920s—the cubist painter, the dadaist dabbler, the daring linguistic experimenter, the ruthless satirist who heaped scorn on American culture." And he concludes, "And how infinitely far seems the E. E. Cummings of the final years, the curmudgeon of Patchin Place who yearned for an older time," the arch-Republican and conservative. Then there are other selves as well—"The libidinous faun of New York and Paris, the Nature lover alert to the presence of her winged, footed, leaved, and petaled creatures, the spellbinding poetry reader widely acclaimed by a generation of college students, and the mystic attuned to a oneness beyond his coherent expression." There are other selves whose story Kennedy also tells, and we shall be particularly concerned here with the ambivalent sexual self, the tormented lover self, and the bewildered parent self, especially as they relate to the struggling artist self.

II

The next three chapters deal with Cummings' forebears, his parents, and his childhood and boyhood. Most significant are his parents and his early and continuous devotion to writing and drawing. His father, Edward, was a physically and personally imposing man, "a striver, a leader, a fighter," as Kennedy describes him, and "Because of this basic difference in temperament," he speculates, "there was bound to be more conflict than usual between father and son when the boy reached his teens." After taking his master's in the Harvard Divinity School, Edward continued with graduate studies in sociology, and then traveled and studied in Europe. Comments Kennedy, "he was probably the best trained sociologist in the United States," and in 1891 he became "the first instructor in sociology in the history of [Harvard] College." "In our day," Kennedy says, "he probably would have become a social worker or a bright young man in the Department of Health, Education, and Welfare." He wrote on trade unions, cooperatives, strike arbitration, penal codes, philanthropic institutions, and the social problems of the industrial revolution. "He was active in penal reform and in promoting the probation system, particularly for 'penal aspects of drunkenness.'" He worked at the Hale Settlement House and through this connection became associated with the South Congregational Church. He was, in brief, not only an imposing and active man, he was a reformer, a do-gooder, precisely one of the types Cummings later selected as an object of satire. We will have occasion to speculate about the psychological meaning of this fact further on.

Nevertheless—and it is this aspect of his father which Cummings was able to celebrate more openly—Edward was a devoted and loving family man, and he and his wife, Rebecca Haswell Clarke, together with various relatives and servants, saw to it that Estlin and his younger sister Elizabeth grew up in a large Cambridge home and "in the midst of a model extended family." Rebecca "was a jolly, stout, . . . warm, motherly person, just five feet four inches tall." And she was intensely involved in her children, helping them with reading, writing, drawing, telling stories, and so on. That such a loving background could produce a man with such problems in husbanding and fathering as Cummings had is one of the mysteries of human life, and what he himself praised his parents for[2] was precisely what he was tragically unable to give his own child. But the case, of course, is much more complex that I have made it seem so far, so let us follow Kennedy's story.

Cummings' childhood and boyhood had additionally to do with growing up in Cambridge and attending its schools. He began writing and drawing quite early, grew to love the circus, had playmates, went to Joy Farm in New Hampshire for the summers, and all in all was imbued with the characteristic late-Victorian values of a cultivated, celebrated, insulated, and well-to-do New England enclave. With his mother's encouragement, he began writing verses around six years of age. "Stacks of juvenilia still exist, for Mrs. Cummings saved every scrap," wryly comments Kennedy, the indefatigable researcher. The boy even compiled a volume of his best poems when he was twelve. His poetry, however, up to and including most of his college years, was thoroughly traditional—in the tradition, that is, of Longfellow. At Cambridge Latin School he was strong in languages and weak in math and science, a pattern which he repeated at Harvard. When he was fifteen, his uncle, George Clarke, gave him a book of rhyming, and Cummings began experimenting with forms. He continued to write prolifically.

III

Kennedy devotes chapters 5 and 6 to the Harvard experience. Here Cummings discovered Keats, *The Greek Anthology*, the classical writers, Dante, and English and Continental literature. He also began discovering Boston. And he continued writing, falling now under the spell of Rossetti—which Kennedy says was unfortunate for the young poet. He also points out the other weaknesses of the curriculum of that time in offering very little in the way of critical theory or analytical practice, with the result that Cummings' own critical essays aren't very interesting—a judgment with which I rather disagree. Nevertheless, what Cummings *didn't* get from his formal education—math, science, economics, history—is almost as impressive as what he *did* get.

Yet it is during Cummings' five-year stay at Harvard that Kennedy finds the first significant personality change taking place. At seventeen he wrote a self-description, revealing himself as a scion of the late-Victorian New England ethos, exactly the sort he was later to satirize in "come,gaze with me upon this dome" (*is* 5, Two, VIII). At twenty-two, however, he "was in full rebellion against his father, he hated Cambridge, he scorned the prevailing American attitudes and tastes, and he associated with a lively, spree-drinking, girl-chasing group of young men who were apprentices in the new artistic movements of the twentieth century." He joined the *Harvard Monthly* and found friends in Scofield Thayer, S. Foster Damon, John Dos Passos, J. Sibley Watson, Stewart Mitchell, and Arthur Wilson. What took place in his writing during his final months at Harvard, therefore, was a loosening up—in verse forms, in diction, and in subject matter. He was becoming intensely aware, and wanted to become a part, of the modern movement. He began writing poems which we now recognize as uniquely Cummings' of the *Tulips and Chimneys* period.

And he was trying to distance himself from his father, who was a loving, well-intentioned parent but who was also somewhat too intrusive and controlling. The young man began feeling resentful of his father's sometimes overbearing treatment of his mother, and Kennedy says, "This period of Oedipal crisis was hard on both father and son." And he quotes Cummings' own statement made many years later: "I loved him: first as a child, with the love which is worship; then, as a youth, with the love that gives battle; last, as a man, with the love which understands."

IV

Cummings completed his Harvard studies in 1916, after receiving his master's degree. Kennedy's next five chapters deal with Cummings' subsequent development up to his first serious love relationship. First there is his participation in Mitchell's idea to publish *Eight Harvard Poets* (1917); his realization, under the influence of Ezra Pound, that he could experiment with spacing; and his beginning to use the lower-case "i." Thayer married Elaine Orr, and Watson married Hildegarde Lasall. Thayer commissioned Cummings to write an epithalamion and paid him $1,000 for it, which enabled Cummings to consider moving to New York. Meanwhile he was living at home and writing, consolidating "the basic styles that were to be characteristic of his future work." Kennedy shows him experimenting systematically with visual arrangement and sound patterns and developing his three principal styles: the lyric and mythic, the Satyric, and the Hephaestian (or modernist). Then there is his actual move to New York at the beginning of 1917, where he worked for not quite two months in the office of a mail-order publishing house. He then decided to devote himself entirely to writing and painting—and exploring the city.

The United States entered the European war on April 6, and on April 17 Cummings signed up with the ambulance service. On the passage out, he met William Slater Brown, and the two became inseparable friends for years. They explored Paris together and, although they became familiar with some prostitutes, Cummings remained technically a virgin—partly out of deference to his high-minded background and partly out of fear of venereal disease. And after they were sent into the field, they got into that trouble, resulting in imprisonment, immortally recounted in *The Enormous Room.* "The whole experience gave Cummings an opportunity to know intimately men of classes and nations he never would have encountered anywhere in his life." Naturally, his father, who was head of the World Peace Foundation at that time and who had political connections, offered to help. These words from a letter to his son are revealing: "You poetic and artistic chaps are so afraid of being conventional and commonplace that you often hide your real emotions under a camouflage of words that is sometimes about as difficult to make anything out of as a cubist portrait of a 'Nude descending the stairs.'" There's a good bit of stuffed-shirtism here, and Cummings was indeed involved in exploring the new artistic consciousness, but this passage, as we shall see, is painfully prophetic in some ways of what Cummings himself was to come to realize many years later.

He at first proudly rejected his father's help but was glad enough at the end, after three months, to be released as a result of that very help. On the way home he had two nights in Paris and "was determined not to return to the United States without a fully consummated sexual experience." After arriving home in early 1918, he was urged by his father to write down his experience La Ferté-Macé. He moved back to New York with Slater Brown and resumed writing, painting, and exploring the city. But he was drafted in July and spent six months at Camp Devens, about an hour's ride or less north of Cambridge. Again he refused parental admonitions to apply for officer candidate school, resolved to make his own way, and again he was somewhat beaten by the experience. Yet he was enduring a second period of maturation as a result of these difficult times, and he began formulating his philosophy of life: immediacy of sensation, creativity, uniqueness, primitiveness, freedom, independence, and submission to physical and social reality. It can be seen that the last item could conflict with some of the others, and indeed that turned out to be the case.

He was also going "through another important creative period in his life," and during his free time at camp he read and wrote letters, poems, and essays. And he was developing his aesthetic philosophy as well, particularly that which bears upon mingling the various arts with one another, as Kidder has shown (see chapter 9 above). This theme shows up in his experimentation, à la cubism, with jarring juxtapositions. He was also in a state of erotic turmoil and was writing many of those early sexual poems marked by violent ambivalence. He was discharged, after finally being persuaded by his father to plead financial hardship, early in 1919.

V

Chapters 12–17 deal with what seems to me the central tragedy of Cummings' life and writing—the failure to integrate love and art—which is, in fact, the theme of his play *Him*, and which in all probability is responsible for the ultimate impenetrability of that work and, as he himself was later to suggest, for his difficulty in producing works of any sustained length. What I mean by love here, in relation to Cummings' dilemma, is not simply the worship of a woman but in addition the ability to achieve that stage of psychosexual development where one can be a husband to a woman and a father to their child. This implies, generally speaking, a sufficiently successful resolution of the oedipal conflict. What happened to Cummings, however, as we have seen Kennedy telling it, was that his father was both loving and intrusive, a fateful combination—as Cummings himself says in the published letters (86).

First, there were things about his father he couldn't identify with; and second, paradoxically, his father wouldn't let him make the break. Fearing engulfment, the son had to become the distancer to his father's pursuer—a tactic which had limited success, since he had to turn repeatedly to his father for help. Which in one way is what the distancer is trying to provoke, and in another way keeps him looking for others who will help him without making demands on him. This made Cummings permanently defensive against intrusion, real or imagined, and it is my belief that it is this defensiveness, however necessary at the time to salvage whatever of his manhood he could, which hindered not only the development of his personal relationships but also the poetic embodiment of his philosophy of organicism.

The tragedy begins with his love for Elaine Orr who, as we recall, had married Thayer in 1916. Their marriage was not close, as it turned out, and Thayer allowed her much freedom. As their friend, therefore, Cummings found himself spending time with Elaine, and by 1918 had fallen in love with her. He felt conflicted, of course, and "imposed the pattern of courtly love upon it," as Kennedy sees it. And courtly love itself has something oedipal about it, with the man worshipping the forbidden and therefore unattainable woman, another man's wife. Which is surely one of the basic sources of not only Cummings' but also western man's self-serving idealization of Woman analyzed by Professor Fairley (see chapter 9 above). "He thought of himself as a Lancelot loving a Guinivere, . . . who was married to his liege lord, King Arthur," Kennedy comments. Cummings had been through *The Idyls of the King* more than once in college, and it is not irrelevant that Kennedy previously noted how Cummings once compared his father to Arthur vis-à-vis his mother's Guinivere. A man who keeps falling in love with other men's women—and Cummings did it again with his second wife, as we shall see—may in all probability be perpetually reenacting his inability to resolve the oedipal conflict, looking to displace rather than identify with his father—with what resultant anxieties about retaliation and further engulfment we may imagine. Kennedy observes that the self which emerged in relation to Elaine was the little boy self, "who is wistful, powerless, full of yearning, who indulges in rituals to make wishes come true."

To make a long story short, they became lovers. Elaine discovered she was pregnant in the spring of 1919. Nancy, their child, was born December 20, 1919. But a distance was created; the situation became ambiguous, for, although their friends generally knew the truth, "he was the father of a child he could not acknowledge." Nor did he feel especially obligated, apparently. Their association rekindled, however, during the winter of 1920 and continued off and on for four more years.

*   *   *

Kennedy interrupts the story here to catch up on Cummings' life as a painter and writer during this troubled but productive time. He was finishing *The Enormous Room,* for example, and trying to publish *Tulips and Chimneys.* Then he went to Europe in the spring of 1921 and remained for two-and-a-half years, "a period of wandering, of trying to decide what kind of life he wanted with Elaine, and marking time with his poetry and his painting."

The Thayers were divorced by now, and Elaine and Nancy also came to Paris, where Cummings visited and spent time with them. "But he still preferred the role of lover to that of husband. Thinking of himself as dedicated to 'my work,' he shied away from any permanent ties." When Elaine and Nancy returned to New York in September of 1923, Cummings remained to think things over. Subsequently, he too returned, and in March of 1924 they were married.

It did not change their way of life very much, however, and Elaine still kept up the pretense that Nancy was Thayer's child. It is hard to say whether he fell short of commitment because of his own need to distance himself from the demands of intimacy or of her refusal to allow him to assume his commitment, or whether she refused because he was unable, but the fact nevertheless remains that she sailed once again for Europe in May and fell in love with another man, one Frank MacDermot, onboard ship, and wrote asking Cummings for a divorce. This was, writes Kennedy, "the most devastating psychological blow of his life. For the first time in his life, a challenge arose, so personally overwhelming that he could not rise to meet it with his customary high spirits." So he underwent the third change in personality Kennedy records: "never again was he so exuberantly happy-go-lucky; never again did he possess the unshakable self-confidence of youth." And again he turned to his father for help, trying in vain to get Elaine to change her mind. The divorce went through in December. Kennedy's seventeenth chapter is entitled "The Struggle for Nancy" and details the tortuous struggle he and his parents had in trying to secure some kind of custody agreement regarding the child. The upshot of it was that he and Nancy were to all intents and purposes successfully kept apart, mainly, it appears, because Elaine and her new husband were determined that it should be so. Nancy "grew up not knowing that her mother had once been married to the American poet, E. E. Cummings, or that he and not Scofield Thayer was her real father." We shall come upon the later unraveling of this knot in due course.

VI

Meanwhile, Cummings had met and fallen in love with Anne Barton in 1926, and Kennedy's next four chapters take him through these years. Although unlike Elaine in many ways, she too belonged to another man—a prior commitment to an older man named Douglas who gave her and her daughter by a previous marriage financial support—and Cummings went through similar agonies a second time in trying to win a woman away to be his own. Nevertheless, for a while at least, this relationship helped raise him out of the dumps, and Kennedy says that it was genuinely sexual rather than idealized, nor was Anne "in any way the mothering caretaker." At this time, while he was working on *Him*, he went through the terrible experience of his father's death in an auto accident. He was also reading Freud and entered into a full psychoanalysis with Dr. Fritz Wittels. We can infer some of what he gained from this treatment via some fragmentary notebook jottings Kennedy quotes from this period:

> rebelling *as a child* ("I won't marry because you
> want me to")
> If I could *stop fighting* with my father (dead) about
> marriage I *could fight* with the substitutes for my
> father (alive) e.g. MacDermot, [Peter Finley] Dunne
> I have never grown up
> assumed the responsibilities of a man
> I have preferred to have a mistress because it
> won't hurt me so much when I lose her (as, a wife)
> I won't fight for her.
> to help her.

Apparently encouraged by this treatment to make a commitment, he married Anne in the spring of 1929. In 1931, while he and Anne were in Europe, he made the trip to Russia on which *Eimi* is based. Anne also discovered she was pregnant and returned to New York for an abortion. Obviously there were strains on both sides; Anne became attracted to another man, and their marriage came apart in 1932.

Eimi came out in 1933, and Kennedy finds this work representative of a fourth change in Cummings: "He grew more deeply committed to his philosophy of life when he saw how it could be threatened by a governmental system. The energy that he devoted to expressing his values in *Eimi* strengthened him in his defense of individualism so that he became much more confident and assertive in his views—in time, even dogmatic." At length, he came to despise not only communists but also liberals—this, of course, during those years when the West was struggling out of the Great Depression. And could we not add that his emerging conservatism had also something to do with the loss of his father within the same six-year period that he lost a wife a second time to another man? Cummings was now almost forty years old, and the need to achieve a more stable identity was imperative.

VII

The next six chapters take him into his full maturity. But it is significant that, even here at the beginning of chapter 22, Kennedy quotes him as reflecting back on his emotional state after his break with Anne and saying that loss and separation are "intolerable" for him, and yet that something positive usually emerges to take the place of the missing "parent or relative, perhaps . . . a girl with whom I've been . . . entirely in love." While Kennedy sees this introspection as a sign of Cummings' resilience, and uses it as a way of leading into the introduction of Marion Morehouse in the poet's life in 1932, it can also be seen as a sign of the profound and unresolved problem Cummings had with closeness, distance, and boundaries. At any rate, Marion was destined to be with him for the final thirty years of his life, and "she became the person who filled his every need. She played the role of mistress, mother, housekeeper, nurse, hostess, cook, accountant, model, courier, secretary, muse, and a great many other parts in a lifelong companionship." In return, he was worshipful of her. She was beautiful, a high-fashion model, and regal, and apparently in their mutual devotion she found *her* life's fulfillment.

And it seems to me that even Cummings' mature love poetry—*especially* that poetry—is marked by the same feeling of reverencing an ideal in the woman as he had in relation to Elaine. Indeed, in some ways all of Cummings' serious love poems are written about that same ideal, regardless of which actual woman they were inspired by. However, Kennedy's pointing out which poems were inspired by which woman deserves further investigation.

Kennedy then relates the story of *No Thanks*, published in 1935, commenting on a new religious tone appearing therein, "a further development of the tendency revealed at the end of *Eimi.*" He says Cummings was not a Christian but was perhaps feeling more conciliatory about the memory of his father as well as responding to Marion's influence. My own opinion is that he was feeling more comfortable about himself and thus more able to plumb the depths of his other, less "political" self, his Taoist self, and that this self owes as much to his warm and accepting mother as to his religious and reformer father. *No Thanks* was, after all, dedicated to his mother— who had advanced the money for its publication. Kennedy quotes the following from Cummings' notes: "her spirit expressed joy alone and nothing but joy, joy . . . as if, when the man who is her son takes her in his arms, she can feel his unborn wish kicking at her heart." This is as vivid a description of mother-child symbiosis as can be imagined.

Cummings and Marion made a fruitless and frustrating trip to Hollywood, and upon their return he was engaged in equally fruitless and frustrating attempts to get *Tom* produced. And he was losing touch with many of his literary and artistic friends of the 1920s because of his anti-liberalism, fearing that Roosevelt's program of social reform was leading the United States down the road to Moscow. His recognition as a writer, however, started really to grow with the publication in 1938 of *Collected Poems.* He began to be invited to give poetry readings and was writing some of his most memorable poems. One was "my father moved through dooms of love" (*50 Poems*, #34), which, Kennedy says, "represents a real psychological breakthrough." And he continues, "He seems to have removed some restriction from his deepest self, a release which then allowed him to identify himself with his father, for he even transfers to duty-filled Edward Cummings his own self-directed philosophy of life," and he quotes, "Scorning the pomp of must and shall / my father moved through dooms of feel." If we agree with the latter part of this statement, and I think it is correct, then I don't see how we can agree with the former part, for transferring one's *own* traits to another is hardly to identify with that person—it is, rather, to identify that person with oneself. Or, in this case, it is more as if Cummings were transferring his *mother's* traits to his father. However this may be, "Cummings felt that it was the beginning of a new poetic period for him, one in which he spoke with a more responsible, morally concerned tone."

As World War II was beginning overseas, he published 50 *Poems* and was starting to have health problems, needing a specially designed corset to ease the pain of arthritis in his spine. Kennedy comments that this and similar physical limitations and pains must have contributed to Cummings' growing irritability, not to mention the effect of Marion's falling seriously ill with arthritis herself during these years. Yet he continued somehow to be creative and productive, publishing 1 x 1 in 1944 and *Santa Claus* in 1946. It seems evident that some of his long-buried feelings about Nancy found expression in this latter work, and as it happened, these feelings were prophetic—though not of how things actually turned out.

VIII

Kennedy's final five chapters are decisive as far as our quest to understand Cummings' struggle is concerned, and they do, of course, take him to the end of his life and career. Marion and he became increasingly more dependent on one another, and "Marion's role as protector and caretaker seemed to enlarge as Rebecca Cummings had less involvement in her son's life," for his mother was in her late eighties and died in 1947. Nancy was twenty-six in 1945 and married, and although she still did not know that Cummings was her father, she had learned that he had been married at one time to her mother. Having spent a good deal of her childhood and youth abroad, she was in the United States during the war years and somehow managed to meet Cummings in the autumn of 1946. By 1947 she had two children—Simon, born in 1945, and Elizabeth, 1947—and was in the habit of visiting Cummings on occasion and sat for him as he painted her.

On one of these visits in 1948 the conversation turned to her "father," Scofield Thayer, and after a pause, Cummings finally said, "Did anyone ever tell you I was your father?" Nancy, at first stunned, of course, was delighted and wanted to become, along with her children, a part of his "family," but Marion was positively jealous. "Marion herself had wanted to have a child, but Cummings would not let her." She in turn became increasingly more protective, shielding him from practicalities—even, Kennedy says, "from life itself, so that he became less able to bear the stresses of the outside world." In response to the advances of his newly acknowledged daughter, who was now engaged in a struggle to secure a father which very much resembled his own struggle to secure a daughter years before, Cummings was prompted to question the very self he had by now become: "it seems to me that she is real, & my life here (with M) isn't. What are all my salutings of [Mount] Chocorua [at sunset] & worshipping of birds & smellings of flowers & fillings of humming bird cups, etc. They're sorry substitutes for human intercourse generally & particularly[,] for spiritual give-&-take with a child or a child-woman whom I adore—someone vital & young—& gay!"

But at the same time he found himself resisting for fear "of being made into a bon bourgeois; for fear of the 'respectable' collectivity, of the makers of categories & pigeonholes." Yet he was questioning himself again in 1950, and Kennedy says these "statements are those of a very pathetic human being, made so partly by what the world had done to him and partly by what he himself had done to bring about the world's reaction." This is what Cummings says, and it represents the key to our search: "since Nancy's latest visit, am feeling: O, for such a love! The lack of it is what makes me write merely short poems: keeps me from achieving great works: when the EO-N [Elaine Orr-Nancy] thread broke, I broke too. Since then, have been lost in a fragmentary world (my'unworld'!) of abstraction & generalities, of hatreds & scorns & satires, of la vie politique et pratique et toujour banale." Far from revealing a pathetic human being, however, it seems to be that these statements reveal a searing self-awareness—an awareness that one's limits as an artist can be in some ways related to one's limits as a human being.

It was too late for Cummings and Nancy, however, too late for him to unbecome what he had so painstakingly become, and their relationship cooled. Let us pause for a moment to consider the meaning of this playing out of what I have called the central tragedy of Cummings' life. Somewhat later on, Kennedy discusses Cummings' many frustrated attempts to write another full-length play and speculates on why he seemed unable to sustain a major literary structure. Even *The Enormous Room*, *Him*, *Eimi*, and *Santa Claus*, says Kennedy, and I partly agree, are not fully articulated structures, although he concedes that *Santa Claus* is the most unified. What Kennedy *doesn't* consider is that possible connection between this problem and those moments of introspection quoted above. It seems to me that Cummings himself put his finger on the very cause: in order to write longer works, one must be able to construct a plot out of the interactions among human beings,[3] and in order to do that, one must have insight into "human intercourse generally" and specifically into the "spiritual give-&-take with a child"—or into being a mate and perhaps also a parent—precisely what he himself also defined, in another mood, as being "bourgeois" and hostile to art and the life of the artist.

IX

This confusion, it seems to me, gives the whole game away. In his earlier years, Cummings was limited, self-limited, by his adopting the role of bohemian poet, and in his later years by his adopting the role of bohemian-*moralist* poet, the poet of "hatreds & scorns & satires," and so on. In either case, he was, as he frankly told Nancy, "a wholly selfish individual, whose work—or play—is his life." Thus the artist who protects himself against life for the sake of his art paradoxically ends up by impoverishing not only his life but also that very art he was so anxious to preserve. It was his old fear of engulfment again, that distancing sense of self which needs defenses of iron against a demanding and intrusive love, that self being able to love primarily when at the receiving end of a giving and mothering love.

   This—at least in part—is what kept him "from achieving great works," and this is what creates the cracks, where they appear, in his achieved works—that sense of me-against-the-world, that need to praise one thing by disparaging something else, that very polarization which his own best philosophy avoids: "Never the murdered finalities of wherewhen and yesno,impotent nongames of wrongright and rightwrong."[4] The artist may need to avoid *bourgeois values*, but this is not the same thing, as I have said, as rejecting the normal tasks of *human development* as one grows through the stages of one's life.

   Yeats once wrote that the artist must choose between perfection of the work and perfection of the life, but I do not think he made such a choice himself. If we isolate ourselves so as to be able to write, we may very well run the risk of having little left to write about. It is a torment, this tension, for if we throw ourselves into life, we may waste the time and energy we need to write. But it is a torment which repays struggling with it, for too-easy solutions on either side are not worth the candle.

And it is also paradoxical that the artist who devotes his whole vision to the value of growth should reject a portion of the stages of his own growth. True it is that the artist must preserve a view of life from a standpoint outside of society, and correspondingly that he must preserve an openness to life like that of a child, for he must not become "simply" an "adult," bound to societal routines. But it is also true that this in no way entails an avoidance of commitment and responsibility. A child is a child because he is growing, and if he grows, he must become an adult; an adult who is also growing is like a child in this but not in those other ways. The real trick is to stay alive and growing through the whole thing. Cummings spoke of integrity of the individual self, of being true to that self, but he also spoke of being a whole person, of growth, and of love, not always seeing how the former could oppose the latter when it becomes a holding action, a defensive strategy.

I want to be clear about this: an artist does not literally need to be a spouse and parent to be fulfilled either as an artist or as a human being. I think immediately of Jane Austen, Emily Dickinson, Thoreau, Kafka, Henry James as examples. It is true, of course, that being an artist uses up a lot of one's psychic energy, and it is difficult in a society such as ours to make a living at one's art in order to be able to support or contribute to the support of a family. To survive as an artist under these conditions, one *does* need to protect oneself against invasion, distraction, intrusion, and the dissipation of one's energies. But it does not help to use this necessity to rationalize the rejection of large portions of one's self and one's life. One can remain unmarried and still write insightfully about courtship, marriage, and parenting. One can understand more than one experiences, as I have said, but one needn't write about *less* than one understands. I have no quarrel with Cummings' life—it is neither for me nor anyone else to tell another how to live. I have no quarrel with his understanding, either: he saw himself more clearly than I or Kennedy can see him. My quarrel with him is that he had more understanding than he chose to put into his published writings.

It's not that poetry has to be "confessional." Robert Lowell has certainly been as open as one would care to have anyone be in print about his emotional and psychological problems, his failed marriages, his affairs, his children, and so on, and yet whatever I may think of his work, I do think there are other ways of making one's art responsive to one's actual life. But the point about Cummings is that he made whatever it is that he achieved—and it was, in many ways, "great"—seem less of a struggle than it really was. Had he been able to deal with that struggle more fully, given his already considerable genius, his achievement would have been even greater. What I have in mind, as noted before, is something like *Him,* where he seemed set on confronting the issue, however artfully and disguisedly. Guided by Cummings' own later comments on the play, but long before his letters and papers became more available, I once wrote that the protagonist was "caught between being a divided man—a would-be artist plus a domesticated husband—and becoming a whole man—and therefore an actual artist because he can love," and that "The resolution would not require the artist to abandon his work in order to become a husband—but rather to become a husband in order to become an artist."[5]

Something fatal must have happened to Cummings after he wrote that play, and we recall Kennedy's previous speculations about why he never seemed able to write another one like it. Cummings himself put it in terms of loss, not only of Elaine but even more of Nancy. And of his father. And of his second wife. And the play itself was roundly trounced by the reviewers, both as a theatrical event and as a book. He seems to have cumulatively suffered a mortal wound from which he never wholly recovered. Henceforth he would have to protect himself around the area of this hurt. An artist, a man, a failure—must proceed! But proceed as if nothing has happened? It is not that his avoidance of being a family man did him in; rather, his avoidance of putting into his published work how he tried, how he failed, and what it cost him. One either presents the struggle or rises above it, but one does not pretend that it never happened. If Cummings chose to write from his serene and confident stance, he needn't have satirized so savagely those who failed to achieve that level of transcendence. He tried to have it both ways: he knew how tragically hard it is to sustain one's sense of one's self, and yet he did not seem to appreciate how hard it is for others.

The result is that, where he fails as an artist, he fails through mistakes in emphasis and rhetoric, through confusions between poetry and politics (and he is not the first!), through defining by exclusion, through overinsistence, through oversimplification. That damned defensiveness and self-protectiveness keeps him off balance, creating a poetic hyperbole and then taking it as literal truth. "Thinking" *may* indeed be used to avoid "feeling," but not always or necessarily. He who took such infinite pains both early and late to perfect his art, and who was so conscious of order, structure, technique, style, and effect, as I have said, should not have preached "spontaneity" so casually. He knew very well that true discipline is part of true spontaneity, and indeed it is precisely this knowledge which renders false those accusations of immaturity that hasty critics have been leveling at him almost from the beginning. He himself writes in his published letters how he admires Yeats' "equal understanding of perfectly opposed viewpoints—collective & individual, systematic & spontaneous, rational & instinctive" (255). It is neither very engaging nor convincing to be more aware of others' weaknesses than of one's own, or to have too little sense of the difficulties which even the best and most well-intentioned people have in achieving wholeness and aliveness—which is especially contradictory in a poet who insisted upon the fundamental rightness of Jesus' admonition not to throw the first stone unless you are without sin yourself.[6] The result is sometimes a certain wavering in awareness at the heart of his vision.

X

Much remained to Cummings, however, in the ten or twelve years following the second heartbreak vis-à-vis Nancy. Kennedy details the publication of *Xaipe* in 1950, the Norton Professorship at Harvard during 1952–53, *95 Poems* in 1958, many prizes and awards and readings, and the books that began to be published about him. What we are getting by now, as I hope, is a more accurate grasp of the whole Cummings. What remains to be done is to sort out his faults and his virtues in an objective manner on the one hand, and to continue the effort, as I've tried to show in part 2 above, to broaden the spectrum of modern critical theory and practice on the other. Having traced his transcendentalism partly back to his struggle with his father and incomplete separation from his mother, I have no intention of *reducing* it to that source. The authentic powers of a writer's vision are always more than its personal origins—otherwise it would have little relevance for readers. What I *am* suggesting is that its limits can be seen in terms of that source, and that these limits can help us understand the powers better.

The wonder, then, is not why he couldn't write better; the wonder is rather, given his struggle, that he could write so well. We value him, and must continue to value him, for conveying to us an image of one who encourages us to believe in life while at the same time retaining his own authentic selfhood and artistic uniqueness. We value him for his purity, clar-

ity, musicality, and the complex structuring of his best work. For his manifest delight in language and form. His inventiveness. The pleasure and joy
and fun. Plus what these things reveal of his best feelings and insights: integrity, individuality, love, affirmation, and the importance of feeling, of
being aware, of being in the now, of genuinely being in one's existence.
These themes are not simply important—they are absolutely essential. And
the wonder continues to be that he *did*, despite all, miraculously continue
to grow, moving in his later poetry toward an even deeper and more complex vision. The shock of the final loss of Nancy perhaps opened him up to
that long-shut well of feeling, allowing a renewed sense of self-awareness to
find its way back into his writing, a sense of the reality of pain and limitation—of self-inflicted pain and limitation. We can only be grateful for all
that he *has* given us of himself.

13

Sister Elizabeth and Patroness Hildegarde

This chapter is a review, written originally for *SPRING* (Old Style), June 1985, of the memoirs of two women who were very important in Cummings' life—his sister, and a friend and patroness. *When I was a Little Girl*, by Elizabeth Cummings Qualey, was written during the late 1950s but was not published until some twenty-five years later. *The Edge of the Woods*, by Hildegarde Lasell Watson, with a preface by Bernard N. Schilling, came out in 1979. These writings throw interesting firsthand light on Cummings the youth and the man.

I

The sister's book is dedicated to Elizabeth and Carlton Qualey's adopted children, John and Mary, "and their children and children's children." John and Mary were born in 1940 and 1941, respectively, and Elizabeth used to tell them stories of her childhood before dictating the stories to Carlton in 1957, who then typed them out. Richard Kennedy tells us in *Dreams in the Mirror* (483) that the poet thought they ought to be published and tried to encourage and help her in finding a publisher, but these efforts came to naught. It was finally arranged locally by various sponsors at Madison, New

Hampshire, and the book appeared in its present staple-bound, paper-cover form.

Because it was written for her children, and simply for the sake of showing them what life was like during her childhood, it is a placid, even-toned, and highly detailed description of growing up at 104 Irving Street in Cambridge and at Silver Lake, New Hampshire, during the early years of this century. As part of the upper-middle professional class, the Cummingses had a large house in a pleasant section of Cambridge and a farm and some lakefront property at Silver Lake.

Elizabeth tells of their life in these places, of their servants, their parents, their childhood illnesses and games and playmates, the first horseless carriages, and more. Two items of special interest for readers of her book deserve further comment. The first is her portrait of her older brother Estlin: making due allowances for the fact that he was six or seven years her senior and that she would therefore naturally look up to him, I am still amazed at how capable and competent she portrays him as being. He fixes things, he solves problems, he rides ponies—and most impressively, he saved her from drowning in Silver Lake. Charles Norman, who had the manuscript of Elizabeth's memoir before it was published, recounted this story in *The Magic-Maker* (30–1). They were out on the lake with their dog in a canoe, when it capsized. This would not have been especially dangerous, except that the dog could not swim all the way to shore and returned in a panic, trying to hold onto Elizabeth. Cummings had to drown the dog to save his sister. This sturdy young fellow is a far cry from the "Peter Pan" who keeps cropping up in Kennedy's book, the one who didn't know how to arrange for their bags when he and Elaine were at a hotel, for example, or who could not, at the last, accept Nancy and her children as his family. The young Cummings was, in fact, somewhat like his father, who could fix or build anything at a moment's notice—and he was that young man who did, after all, survive a rather nasty term of imprisonment in France. Something changed him further on.

Which may be related to the second item of interest: Elizabeth's published description of their parents is as unstintingly admiring as Cummings'. It often happens that siblings' accounts of the same parents come out quite differently, but such is not the case here. Mother and father were warm, strong, human, and supportive to all concerned. Never a cross word, never an argument or a fight, never a conflict, never a punishment. Thus Elizabeth's picture corroborates Cummings', especially in his pair of poems on his parents—"if there are any heavens" (W [*ViVa*], #XLIII) and "my father moved through dooms of love" (50 *Poems*, #34)—and in his *i:SIX NONLECTURES* (Nonlecture One).

We may take this corroboration as evidence of accuracy, or as a sign of the investment both children had in the idealized image of their parents. Evidence for the second alternative is found in Cummings' *Selected Letters*, 1922–3, where, as we have seen, he repeatedly urged his younger sister to rebel and leave the parental nest (83–7, 93–5, 101–3). It may be that these parents were "too good," that they were too nurturing and supportive, and that their children did have trouble in separating from them. Whatever normal anger and frustration they may have felt was simply not to be expressed in public: how *can* one, after all, be mad at perfect parents?

Additional evidence is found in the unpublished letters, and here I am pleased to thank Richard Kennedy for lending me his notes and transcripts concerning the correspondence between Elizabeth and Estlin. In addition to the aforementioned crisis surrounding her attempts at separation during the 1920s is the one concerning her own children's adolescence during the middle and late 1950s. John was having a difficult time, and his father appears to have been rather unsympathetic. In addition, Carlton seems to have tried to keep Mary tied to him precisely as Elizabeth's father did to her. Cummings, on the other hand, was quite sympathetic to John, and Elizabeth acknowledged how her brother helped *her* to separate when she was young. Cummings and Elizabeth, in other words, both recognized in private, despite their public adulation, the parallels between these intergenerational conflicts and commented insightfully on the possessiveness of their own parents.

Thus, to backtrack a bit, it may be that older brother became "a small eye poet," an artistic rebel glorying in his unique individuality and aiming satiric barbs at societal reformers and do-gooders (like his father), as his only way out of this curious dilemma. Sadly, however, as we have noticed, he still needed his father to rescue him from several tight spots he had gotten himself into—from La Ferté-Macé, for example, or from the emotional and legal chaos into which Elaine's rejection had thrown him.

I do not think, however, that such issues of family life have necessarily to do with Cummings' genius as an artist. They have to do, rather, with his human fallibilities. But to the extent that these fallibilities affect his art adversely, they are of concern to us. Surely the greatness of his art lies in the loveliness of his love poems, in the vividness of his rural and urban landscapes, and in the bite of his satires, but at times the love poems carry traces of that unresolved idealization, transferred now to his lady, while the satires at times carry traces of that unresolved anger, transferred now to society. Had he been able to retain more of that sturdy manliness of his youth which his sister depicts so clearly, and for which his father served as the natural model, his genius might have been able to fulfill itself even more deeply.

II

Hildegarde Watson was to become another of his rescuers, and her portrait of him in his manhood, interestingly, is as positive as Elizabeth's in his child-hood. She met him, we assume, because she married his well-to-do Harvard friend, James Sibley Watson, who, with another Harvard friend, Scofield Thayer, published the *Dial*, in which some of Cummings' early poetry and drawings appeared. Scofield Thayer, as we know, married Elaine Orr, later Cummings' first wife and the mother of his daughter Nancy.

The Edge of the Woods is a beautiful book, both in its physical appear-ance and in its style. It is also beautiful in its contents, for it tells the story, in Bernard Schilling's words, of her "gilded life as the highborn maiden" (xii). He comments: "Here is the record of a day now spent, of possibilities given to the fortunate ones in late nineteenth- and early-twentieth-century America—of the chance to live in a certain manner under certain assump-tions, to pursue one's own 'Bildung' as the Germans say, toward the fulfill-ment achieved by a truly exceptional person" (ix). So we read of her school-ing in Europe—studying music, art, and literature—of the famous people she mingles with, of her family's vacations in Maine, and so forth.

It is her friendship with Cummings, however, which concerns us here. The first encounter she narrates is when he returned from La Ferté-Macé in 1918. "When he finally returned to New York, his mother and Sibley met him at the boat and brought him, carrying little else but a few notebooks, to 127 East 19th Street. I met him at the door, a hardly recognizable Estlin—in tatters, saddened, and ill" (86). In view of the buoyancy with which he tells of his sufferings in France, we tend, I think, to underestimate what it must have cost him.

Later on she's discussing Marianne Moore's hands, and she says: "Hands have always fascinated me. Estlin Cummings' hands were heart-shaped, like those we see in Persian miniatures, with unbelievably tiny fingertips. His hands were the smallest, I think, I ever saw on a man, but had great strength and adroitness. He seemingly could do anything with them—chop wood, as on his farm in New Hampshire, use the smallest brushes when painting with the accuracy of an artist from the Orient, or tie and untie the littlest knots, something which he liked to demonstrate, laughing as he did so" (132).

Further on she describes the Cummingses' Patchin Place apartment in Greenwich Village, Marion's wonderful cooking, and Estlin's skill at peeling fruit—"like Renoir, one of his favorites, [he] could peel a pear on a fork, deftly cutting off little pieces with a silver knife to hand around for dessert" (143). Also, "He was a sensitive conversationalist, a great talker but also an intense listener" (143). Then she talks about his finances: "E. E. Cummings, in his twenties, had tried many jobs unsuccessfully. At first it upset him—he thought he was inferior; but then he decided it was, after all, an asset. He received a small income and stuck to it—to remain the strong individualist, never to change a word for publisher or public. His splendid smile was never ingratiating. He lived simply as a modern Thoreau whom he greatly admired and urged me to read" (143).

This "small income" came in part through a family inheritance and in part through the Watsons themselves—which she is apparently too modest to mention but which is attested to, as we noted in chapter 10 above, in his published letters of the late 1930s. One wonders what he would have done without these supports, just as one wonders the same thing about Thoreau. Can one really claim to be bringing existence down to its essentials if one has a rescuer waiting in the wings? Does such a one really have the right to scorn "materialism" and chasing after money? Cummings touched upon such questions in his introduction to the 1934 Modern Library edition of *The Enormous Room,* indicating that he did know what it was like to go hungry. This is, of course, true, but the fact remains that, like many well-off Americans escaping their money-grubbing culture, he had nothing ultimately to worry about because there was always a safety net somewhere. But what would it cost to be uncompromising if one had no safety nets anywhere?

Mrs. Watson next shows Cummings giving his "now famous Harvard Non-Lectures," and she describes his "flawless performance. He strolled in with that elegant, erect bearing of his that expressed so well his apparent remoteness, especially noticeable when he was on the lecture platform. To some of the audience, this casualness was maddening; to others of us his indifference appeared heroic, an essential part of the magic of his personality. No one was ever seen to leave his readings" (144).

She then tells of a visit to Joy Farm and finally of visiting the Cummingses in Paris. "That evening, as we were talking about integrity, I told him what a friend had written me — 'No one knows anybody and least of all himself'. Estlin said: 'Poetry is the moment when you feel you are nobody but yourself.'" She concludes: "I heard of his death that fall through a cablegram from my husband. I was in Athens, in the country Cummings cared for most of all. There was a young moon over the Acropolis. Marianne Moore said the most touching thing: 'I feel lonely without him'" (146).

III

What can *we* conclude? That this is indeed, as Schilling suggests, a lost way of life, a way in which privileged and insulated people tried to confront suffering through experience as well as art, to be honest and open while maintaining their inborn reticence, and who succeeded or failed to the extent that anyone succeeds or fails in balancing those three chairs above the audience with or without a net — succeeds or fails in solving our common human problem of growing up in a family and then trying to leave it and become, as Cummings says, nobody but yourself. This is a harder job than he was able to admit to himself, and he covered over the unfinished parts, as most of us have to do, with various jerry-built structures — only the structures he had available to him were somewhat finer and more protective than most of us can lay claim to nowadays.

part

four

:conclusion

14

The Objective Correlative Revisited

Previously unpublished, this chapter suggests ways in which we can profit from a sympathetic awareness of a poet's limitations as well as of his strengths.

I

The result, then, of Cummings' decision not to integrate the negative way more fully into his art—however fully he could treat it in his private writings—was that characteristic polarization: the you-and-me-against-mostpeople stance. What we cannot handle within ourselves, we project outwards. What Cummings could not deal with in himself was, as it seems to me, the unfinished oedipal struggle, which I spoke of in chapter 5: the need for the son to free himself from his primary bond with his mother and to identify with his father instead. His lifelong attachment to his mother, his belated discovery of sex, his often split image of woman as whore or madonna, and his rejection of a manly role in his first marriage and in the world and his identification of his art with that rejection, his opposition to many of the things his father stood for—social reform, for one—all these phenomena point consistently to an unresolved anxiety about his identity. It is a struggle, as I point out in that chapter, to firm up a wavering sense of self.

To be sure, all this psychologizing does not necessarily invalidate his social criticism or his art: the former is often on target, and the latter is frequently brilliant. What it does do is help define the limitations, as well as the powers, of his vision and art. And the limitations of his vision seem to have engendered certain limitations in his art.

Thus, if Cummings' social criticism is frequently cogent, it is partly weakened by the force of his projection: the virulence of some of it diminishes its potential effectiveness—as, for example, in "THANKSGIVING (1956)" (95 *Poems*, #39), or "F is for foetus (a" (*Xaipe*, #37). It is much more convincing—as he himself pointed out to Pound—if the satirist avoids alienating his audience, saying in effect that we are all human and have a share in humanity's usual failings, as well as that it's crucial to spot them and do what we can to remedy them. So too is his love poetry truly inspiring, but it is also partially weakened by its too-heady striving for perfection: love *is* the every only god, but it also involves difficulties, and sometimes children and (if we are very lucky!) even grandchildren.

Cummings' art too is undeniably brilliant: he was not simply an innovator, he was also truly a creator; not simply an experimenter, he was also firmly rooted in the traditions of his art, his culture, and his language. But it is also sometimes similarly weakened by over-emphasis, unnecessary polarization, and self-confessed difficulties with planning and executing larger forms and longer works. Keeping his life clear of responsibilities except to his art may have hampered that very art, as he himself suspected.

II

As it was, he came out bravely enough, and we cannot underestimate, as I have suggested, the value of his relationship with Marion Morehouse in helping him survive and continue on with his life-project. What he *did* manage to enlarge and deepen—and this is my particular emphasis, what survives all the doubts, what seems most of permanent value—is his vision of transcendence. I believe I have done much to help clarify what this is about, and I do hope that it has had and will have a salutory effect upon his reception and reputation. I need only say here that it relates Cummings truly and accurately to the basic romantic tradition out of which the many branches of modernism and postmodernism come—just as it helps rejoin modernism and postmodernism to romanticism and Victorianism, topics which I've dealt with in several of the preceding chapters.

My experience of other Cummings interpreters, both in person as well as in print, shows me clearly that there are many Cummingses—"which world?" he asked in *Eimi*—"I live in so many." Some like to focus on his experimentalism, others on the erotic poetry, still others on the humor and wit—more papers are yet to be written on his nature poetry, his poems for and about children, about sex, about the city, and so on. Although any and all of these topics are of interest to me, "my" Cummings is the "Zen monk" who was so sarcastically dismissed by David Perkins in his *History of Modern Poetry*, and all I can do is to make my case as effectively as I can.

If Cummings was sometimes overly defensive vis-à-vis society and its ills, he was frequently able to open himself utterly to Nature herself and thereby to gaze into the very heart of the mystery. It is here that he is able to accept and transcend the polarities, and it is here that I for one find what I need. For we don't have to be "mature" or "responsible" in order to experience and embody such moments; in fact, it helps enormously, as Wordsworth, among others, discovered, if we have retained something of the freshness of the child's vision. It is precisely here that Cummings' "defects" enable his virtues, and it is not irrelevant that such a vision is entirely compatible with a close identification with one's mother.

In other words, if we regard Cummings' case as exemplifying the problem, in Robert Frost's words, of what to make of a diminished thing—as a matter of recouping his losses after his wartime experience, his divorce from Elaine, his separation from Nancy, the death of his father, the furor over his first and only major effort for the theater, his difficulty in finding publishers, his failed second marriage—we may be better able to understand and accept his subsequent need to shore up his defenses, while at the same time being able to appreciate all that he *was* able to rescue from the wreck.

We must also remember that he was in analysis—even as Eliot was—long before it became a common thing to do. Although Freud was becoming known in this country during the twenties and thirties, in particular among the literati, psychotherapy did not become widespread until after World War II and all the stresses and pressures it engendered. One thinks also, in mentioning Frost, of the terrible personal tragedies *he* and *his* family underwent, and one recalls noticing a certain lack of development in *that* poet's work as well, a certain hardening of attitudes and styles as his career unfolded. Nor do I feel confident that we can value Eliot's later work in verse drama as much as we do his prior career in poetry itself.

Seen from this perspective, what Cummings did may be regarded more in terms of accomplishment than of its lack. He could have, after all, given up entirely and gone into some other way of life. As it was, he kept most of his personal pain to himself, confiding it mainly to his notebooks, and went on with his chosen work—chosen, apparently, since childhood—with all the energy at his disposal. If that work and life became unnecessarily circumscribed in the process, it was the price he paid for his sanity.

III

The really curious thing, however, is that it is exactly in the published works that he characteristically insists on the necessity of openness and of feeling. It was Cummings himself who said, "Almost anybody can learn to think or believe or know, but not a single human being can be taught to feel. Why? Because whenever you think or you believe or you know, you're a lot of other people: but the moment you feel, you're nobody-but-yourself" ("A Poet's Advice to Students," A *Miscellany Revised*, 335).

It is true that a feeling must be experienced or else it isn't a feeling; however, it does not follow that this cannot be taught—or at least that one cannot learn it. If our feelings have become blocked, they are nevertheless still there. It seems reasonable to assume, and I can almost think that Cummings might have agreed, that our capacity for feeling is inborn, although it can become blocked or distorted when we are children by improper parental handling, as well as by a society which places little market value on our authentic inner life. The job of therapy, then—and also of art—is to help us remove the blocks, to weather the difficult and painful process of lifting the repression, and to integrate the newly awakened emotional part of ourselves into the functioning of the organism as a whole.

No simple matter in therapy, even less so in art. Poets sometimes tend to put as many defenses between themselves and their readers as they intend to take down—and Cummings is certainly open, as we have seen, to this charge—or else they try, in the manner of the confessional poets, to be so open and direct about themselves, their lives, their neuroses, and their therapy that they lose the whole point about art—and therapy—in the first place. The tragic fact that some of them ultimately committed suicide should help us see that self-exposure is not the same as self-awareness, that confession is not the same as therapy—confusions not entirely absent from "the talking cure" itself. We don't necessarily master our sickness by making art out of it, as D. H. Lawrence thought, and F. Scott Fitzgerald realized that we can be smarter in our books than in our lives. It is an illusion that we can be our own therapists: without the therapist, we lack the control, the direction, and the holding environment necessary to provide the curative objectivity and transference framework. Poetry by itself, whether for the writer or the reader—teaching by itself—is simply not sufficient.

IV

I do not pretend to know all the answers: we each, poets and readers, must find our own way. On the one hand, I appreciate Frost's "one can see what will trouble this sleep of mine" ("After Apple-Picking"), or "I have it in me so much nearer home/ To scare myself with my own desert places," for example, but I wonder if he's being a bit *too* allusive, a bit overly reticent. Compare the similar effect in Cummings'

> a total stranger one black day
> knocked living the hell out of me—
>
> who found forgiveness hard because
> my(as it happened)self he was
>
> —but now that fiend and i are such
> immortal friends the other's each
> (95 *Poems*, #58)

—this from the last book of poems he published while alive. On the other hand, then, we may feel we are being a bit teased, that we could use a *little* bit more information, that the artistic frame is a bit too tight.

Some insight may be gained by comparing poetry and therapy in this regard. If the proper method of therapy is to discharge the repressed emotion onto its appropriate object—more accurately, its object-representation in the psyche—and not simply to let it all hang out, then the job of the poet, as Eliot suggested in his 1919 essay on *Hamlet* (and I am not sure that his use of psychological insight has as yet been fully appreciated), is to find an appropriate object in terms of which to embody the emotion. One difference, however, is that the poetic object may be invented and not necessarily literally true to the poet's actual experience—what needs to be true is the *emotion*. Indeed, so emphatic was Eliot at that time in avoiding mere subjectivity that he insisted that the poet abjure personal feelings entirely. It seems to me that Browning in his dramatic monologues, for example—

which account for most of his poetry—developed an extraordinarily effective way of objectifying the subjective.

Yet the lyric need not be abandoned, either. Behind Eliot is Keats' notion of negative capability, and behind that is the Japanese theory of the haiku. Working on a way of formulating structurally the difference between a poem of self-indulgence *versus* one of self-awareness, I've been using a version of the psychological phenomenon of projection for the purpose. When the speaker of a poem contemplates an object in the external world, for example, he may either surround it with his feelings or strive to see the object in itself, or perhaps move from the former to the latter in taking back the projection.

Although we must acknowledge that such distinctions are matters of degree rather than of kind, there *is* nevertheless a difference, artistically, between the chameleon-poet and the egotistical-sublime. In Frost's "Come In," for example, the speaker, after interpreting the thrush's song as being "Almost like a call to come in / To the dark and lament," decides he would not come in, "not even if asked, / And I hadn't been." It's interesting to relate this poem to Keats' "Nightingale" and Hardy's "Darkling Thrush." In all three cases the speaker balances between the projection and taking it back: at the conclusion of "Nightingale," the speaker loses his consolatory vision, comes back to reality, and wonders if he's been dreaming; in the Hardy poem, the speaker simply can't identify with the bird's song to begin with, being able only to experience his separateness from it.

I think that it is *this* structural feature—respect for the separateness of the object—rather than any simply technical device such as concreteness, indirection, symbolism, irony, and so on, which distinguishes successful lyric embodiment from what T. E. Hulme and the early Pound liked to call emotional slither, or what the New Critics called sentimentality—what Eliot called emotion in excess of the object (although he was so spectacularly mistaken about *Hamlet*, his primary illustrative example).

What we need, then, are two things: self-awareness, and the ability to embody it in artistic form. And the problem is that an otherwise major poet, such as Ezra Pound, for example, may have more than enough of the latter but too little of the former. Or, as I have noted, the poet may be uncertain about the boundary between self-exposure and self-awareness. The case of Cummings, I am suggesting, is especially curious, because he had more than enough self-awareness but too little confidence in his ability to put it into his published work. He himself acknowledged that this had two main detrimental effects on his art: his positive and negative attitudes are too often simply polarized, thereby encouraging him to project the negative outwards; and his ability to create larger forms and longer works was somewhat hampered thereby. And indeed it is not clear that Pound himself mastered these problems, despite his dogged persistence in keeping up with the *Cantos* and enduring the personal suffering involved.

V

What all this shows, then, is that, if we are active readers rather than passive, we can learn as much from a poet's limitations as from his virtues. We must enter into a dialogue with our best writers and look for them to toe the mark. Rather than merely imbibing wisdom, we should engage in vital interaction with them. What they fail to provide, we must summon up from within our very being and call them into account. In that process we can find new ways to grow—one of Cummings' favorite words—and thank them for their help. For me, this means a search for new ways of teaching and writing about poetry, and I can only feel grateful to Cummings for helping me to look for some of those ways—as much in what he didn't as in what he did provide.

> rain or hail
> sam done
> the best he kin
> till they digged his hole
>
> :sam was a man
>   (1 X 1, #XXVIII)

Chapter Two: Cummings Posthumous I

1. "The Old Man Who Said 'Why,'" *Harvard Wake* no. 5 (Spring 1946): 5–8; "A Little Girl Named I," *Wake* no. 6 (Spring 1948): 3–5; "The House That Ate Mosquito Pie," *Wake* no. 9 (Autumn 1950): 5–7. I gather that the "Harvard" was dropped from the title of the journal after the editor, Seymour Lawrence, graduated. "The Elephant and the Butterfly" appears to have been written much later than the other three, contrary to the dedication. See chapter 2, note 4.

2. Reck points this out in his review of *Fairy Tales*, 562.

3. Norman, *Poets & People*, 66.

4. Richard Kennedy writes me that "Cummings was working on 'The Elephant and the Butterfly' while Nancy was visiting him at Silver Lake, after their reunion; the date seems to be summer 1950."

5. Cowley, "Cummings: One Man Alone."

6. Norman, *Poets & People*, 304–6.

7. Norman, 236. The first edition is *The Magic-Maker: E. E. Cummings*, 1958.

8. See Jacobsen, "Legacy," and Triem, *E. E. Cummings*, 42–43.

9. See Gregory's review of *73 Poems*.

10. Tanner, in "Grammar of Poetry," compares Cummings' shock tactics to the sense of the absurd we find in William Burroughs.

11. Abel comments on this poem in his review of *73 Poems*.

12. "You aren't Mad, Am I," Cummings' essay on burlesk (1925), is reprinted in *A Miscellany*, revised edition, 126–31. See also Mullen, "Cummings and Popular Culture."

13. Cline, "Whole Cummings."

14. Tucker, "Cummings the Chivalrous."

15. Donahue, "Cummings' Last Poem."

Chapter Four: Hopkins, Cummings, and the Struggle of the Modern

1. Gardner, *Hopkins*, 265–66.

2. Bender, *Hopkins*.

3. Wain, "Idiom."

4. Deutsch, *Poetry in Our Time*, 111–16.

5. Press, *Chequer'd Shade*, 14–15.

6. Miller, *Disappearance*, 270–359.

7. Ibid., 359.

8. Cummings, *Collected Poems* (1938), introduction.

9. Quoted in Miller, *Disappearance*, 309.

10. Ibid., 359.

Chapter Five: The Two Cummingses

1. Wagner-Martin, "Cummings' *Him*—and Me."
2. Friedman, *Growth of a Writer*, 57–58.
3. Cowley, ed., *Whitman's "Leaves,"* editor's introduction.

Chapter Six: Cummings and His Critics

1. The original article on which this chapter is based concluded with over ten pages of bibliography, arranged chronologically by decades and according to whether the items were favorable, unfavorable, or mixed. However, it didn't seem necessary or suitable for the purposes of this book to include all this very detailed material. The bibliography herein lists extensive scholarly resources which have become available since then—most notably Rotella's invaluable work discussed below in chapter 9—but if the reader should wish to consult the omitted lists, she or he will find them in the spring 1964 issue of *Criticism* wherein the original version was published.

2. Kermode, *Romantic Image*; Langbaum, *Poetry of Experience*; Bayley, *Romantic Survival*; Krieger, *New Apologists*; Foster, *New Romantics*.

3. Quoted in Norman, *Magic-Maker*, 340.

Chapter Seven: Beyond Villains and Heroes?

1. Merton, *Chuang Tzu*, 91. Compare also McNaughton, *Taoist Vision*.
2. Frankenberg, *Pleasure Dome*, 183ff.
3. Tucker, "Cummings the Chivalrous," 25–7.
4. Merton, *Chuang Tzu*, 91.

Chapter Nine: Further Developments in Cummings Criticism

1. Garcia Villa, ed., *Harvard Wake*; Norman, *Magic-Maker*; Firmage, *Cummings Bibliography*; Friedman, *Cummings Art*; Baum, ed., *ΕΣΤΙ*; Marks, *Cummings*; Friedman, *Growth of a Writer*; Wegner, *Poetry and Prose*; Grossman, *Cummings*; Attaway, *Cummings' Aloofness*; Triem, *Cummings*; Eckley, *Merrill Checklist* and *Merrill Guide*; Friedman, ed., *Cummings Critical Essays*; Dumas, *Cummings Remembrance*; Fairley, *Cummings and Ungrammar*; Lane, *I Am*; Kennedy, ed., *Journal of Modern Literature*; Kidder, *Cummings Introduction*; Rotella, *Cummings Reference Guide*; Kennedy, *Dreams in the Mirror*.

2. McBride published her *Concordance* in 1989.

3. Rotella has indeed continued his bibliography in *Resources for American Literary Studies* and *SPRING*. See also Wagner-Martin, *Resources for American Literary Studies*.

4. *Selected Letters*, 225.

5. Although Kidder has not published a book on Cummings' art, Cohen lists four additional articles by him in *E. E. Cummings' Paintings*, 16. Additionally, Cohen's subsequent book, *POETandPAINTER*, should be consulted.

Chapter Ten: Cummings Posthumous II

1. See Kennedy, "Edward Cummings," 437–9; Mott, "Cummings Two Texts"; Cowley, "Cummings Man Alone"; Dumas, *Cummings Remembrance*, 16–17.

2. See "Scourge of the Unpeople," *Times Literary Supplement*, 1403.

3. Shapiro, review of *Selected Letters*, 4.

Chapter Eleven: Knowing and Remembering Cummings

1. There are 105 letters from 1947 to 1962 in the Cummings collection in the Houghton Library at Harvard.

2. 20 August 1951. Reprinted in Baum, ed., ΕΣΤΙ, 173–82.

3. Friedman, "Poem versus Slogan," 18–23.

4. All quotations from Marion's correspondence are c. 1981, by the estate of Marion M. Cummings.

5. Reprinted in *A Miscellany*, revised edition, "A Foreword to Krazy" (1946), 323–8.

6. Friedman, "Diction, etc.," and "Poetic Mask."

Chapter Twelve: "so many selves"

1. "so many selves" is from *Xaipe*, #11.

2. *i:SIX NONLECTURES*, One and Two.

3. This is not to ignore the entire vexed issue of modernist attempts to write longer works *without* plot—via fragments juxtaposed according to mythic parallels, and so on—but it is not particularly relevant to the point being made here, since Kennedy's description of Cummings' various thwarted attempts indicate that he was wrestling with plots of one kind or another.

4. *Collected Poems* (1938), introduction.

5. Friedman, *Growth of a Writer*, 60, 62.

6. *i:SIX NONLECTURES*, 66–7, referring to John, viii,7.

bibliography

Works of E. E. Cummings

POETRY

All of Cummings' published poetry is found in *Complete Poems, 1904–1962*, edited
by George J. Firmage (New York: Liveright, 1991). The separate volumes are included as follows:

Tulips & Chimneys (1922 manuscript). The shortened first version was published in
1923, with the omitted poems appearing in *& [AND]* and *XLI Poems*, both published in 1925. The present version now includes all of *XLI Poems*, which therefore no longer appears among the titles, and the remaining part of *& [AND]*,
which does.

& [AND] (1925).

is 5 (1926).

W [ViVa] (1931).

No Thanks (1935 manuscript).

New Poems [from *Collected Poems*] (1938).

50 Poems (1940).

1 x 1 [*One Times One*] (1944).

Xaipe (1950).

95 Poems (1958).

73 Poems (1963).

Uncollected Poems (1910–62).

Etcetera: The Unpublished Poems (1983).

PROSE, DRAMA, ART

Adventures in Value. Fifty photographs by Marion Morehouse; text by Cummings.
New York: Harcourt, Brace, and World, 1962.

Anthropos: The Future of Art (1930). Mt. Vernon, N.Y.: Golden Eagle Press, 1944.

CIOPW [charcoal, ink, oils, pencil, watercolor]. New York: Covici-Friede, 1931.

E. E. Cummings: A Miscellany (1958). Revised edition. Edited by George J. Firmage.
New York: October House, 1965.

Eimi. New York: Covici-Friede, 1933.

The Enormous Room (1922). Corrected typescript edition. Edited by George J.
Firmage. New York: Liveright, 1978.

Fairy Tales. With pictures by John Eaton. New York: Harcourt, Brace, and World,
1965.

i:SIX NONLECTURES. Cambridge: Harvard University Press, 1953.

Him [play]. New York: Liveright, 1927.

[No Title]. New York: Covici-Friede, 1930. Dadaist tales and drawings.

Santa Claus [a morality]. New York: Henry Holt, 1946.

Selected Letters of E. E. Cummings. Edited by F. W. Dupee and George Stade. New York: Harcourt, Brace, and World, 1969.

Tom [ballet]. New York: Arrow Editions, 1935.

Secondary Sources

Abel, Lionel. Review of *73 Poems. Nation*, December 14, 1963, 420–21.

Attaway, Kenneth R. *E. E. Cummings' Aloofness: An Underlying Theme in His Poetry.* Pamphlet. Atlanta: Georgia State University, 1969.

Baum, S. V., ed. *ΕΣΤΙ: eec: E. E. Cummings and the Critics.* East Lansing: Michigan State University Press, 1962.

Bayley, John. *The Romantic Survival.* Fair Lawn, N.J.: Essential Books, 1957.

Bender, Todd K. *Gerard Manley Hopkins: The Classical Background and Critical Reception of His Work.* Baltimore: Johns Hopkins University Press, 1966.

Cline, Patricia Tal-Mason. "The Whole E. E. Cummings." In *E. E. Cummings: A Collection of Critical Essays*, edited by Norman Friedman, 60–70. Englewood Cliffs, N.J.: Prentice-Hall, 1972.

Cohen, Milton A. *E. E. Cummings' Paintings: The Hidden Career.* Exhibition catalogue, University of Texas at Dallas and Dallas Public Library, September–November 1982.

———. *POETandPAINTER: The Aesthetics of E. E. Cummings's Early Work.* Detroit: Wayne State University Press, 1987.

Cowley, Malcolm. "Cummings: One Man Alone." In his *A Second Flowering*, 90–113. New York: Viking, 1973.

———, ed. *Walt Whitman's "Leaves of Grass": The First (1855) Edition.* New York: Viking, 1959.

Deutsch, Babbette. *Poetry in Our Time.* New York: Columbia University Press, 1952.

Donahue, Jane. "Cummings' Last Poem: An Explication." *Literatur in Wissenschaft und Unterricht* 3 (1970): 106–8.

Dumas, Bethany K. *E. E. Cummings: A Remembrance of Miracles.* New York: Barnes and Noble, 1974.

Eckley, Wilton. *The Merrill Checklist of E. E. Cummings.* Columbus, Ohio: C. E. Merrill, 1970.

———. *The Merrill Guide to E. E. Cummings.* Columbus, Ohio: C. E. Merrill, 1970.

Fairley, Irene R. *E. E. Cummings and Ungrammar.* New York: Watermill Publishers, 1975.

Firmage, George J. *E. E. Cummings: A Bibliography.* Middletown, Conn.: Wesleyan University Press, 1960.

Foster, Richard. *The New Romantics.* Bloomington: Indiana University Press, 1962.

Frankenberg, Lloyd. *Pleasure Dome: On Reading Modern Poetry.* Boston: Houghton Mifflin, 1949.

Friedman, Norman. "Diction, Voice, and Tone: The Poetic Language of E. E. Cummings." *Publications of the Modern Language Association* 77 (1957): 1036–59.

———. *E. E. Cummings: The Art of His Poetry.* Baltimore: Johns Hopkins University Press, 1960.

———. *E. E. Cummings: The Growth of a Writer.* Carbondale: Southern Illinois University Press, 1964.

———. "Poem versus Slogan: In Defense of E. E. Cummings." *Reconstructionist,* February 22, 1952, 18–23.

———. "The Poetic Mask of E. E. Cummings: Character and Thought of the Speaker." *Literary Review* 2 (1958): 124–44.

———, ed. *E. E. Cummings: A Collection of Critical Essays.* Englewood Cliffs, N.J.: Prentice-Hall, 1972.

Garcia Villa, José, ed. *Harvard Wake* no. 5 (Spring 1946). Cummings number.

Gardner, W. H. *Gerard Manley Hopkins (1844–1899): A Study of Poetic Idiosyncrasy in Relation to Poetic Tradition.* London: Secker and Warburg, 1944.

Gregory, Horace. Review of *73 Poems. Commonweal* 79 (March 13, 1964): 725–26.

Grossman, D. Jon. *E. E. Cummings.* Paris: Pierre Seghers, 1966.

Jacobsen, J. "The Legacy of Three Poets." *Commonweal* 78 (May 10, 1963): 189–92.

Kennedy, Richard S. *Dreams in the Mirror: A Biography of E. E. Cummings.* New York: Liveright, 1980.

———. "Edward Cummings, the Father of the Poet." *Bulletin of the New York Public Library* 70 (1966): 437–39.

———. *E. E. Cummings Revisited.* New York: Twayne, 1994.

———, ed. *Journal of Modern Literature* 7, no. 2 (April 1979). Special Cummings number.

Kermode, Frank. *Romantic Image.* London: Routledge and Kegan Paul, 1957.

Kidder, Rushworth. *E. E. Cummings: An Introduction to the Poetry.* New York: Columbia University Press, 1979.

Krieger, Murray. *The New Apologists for Poetry.* Minneapolis: University of Minnesota Press, 1956.

Lane, Gary. *I Am: A Study of E. E. Cummings' Poems.* Lawrence: Regents Press of Kansas, 1976.

Langbaum, Robert. *The Poetry of Experience.* New York: Random House, 1957.

Marks, Barry A. *E. E. Cummings.* New York: Twayne, 1964.

McBride, Katherine Winters, ed. *A Concordance to the Collected Poems of E. E. Cummings.* Ithaca: Cornell University Press, 1989.

McNaughton, William. *The Taoist Vision.* Ann Arbor: University of Michigan Press, 1971.

Merton, Thomas. *The Way of Chuang Tzu.* New York: New Directions, 1965.

Miller, J. Hillis. *The Disappearance of God.* New York: Schocken, 1965.

Mott, Peter H. "E. E. Cummings: Two Texts on God in Man." Ph.D. diss., Columbia University, 1972.

Mullen, Patrick B. "E. E. Cummings and Popular Culture." *Journal of Popular Culture* 5 (1971): 503–20.

Norman, Charles. *The Magic-Maker: E. E. Cummings.* New York: Macmillan, 1958.

———. *Poets & People.* Indianapolis and New York: Bobbs-Merrill, 1972.

Perkins, David. *A History of Modern Poetry: Modernism and After.* Cambridge: Harvard University Press, 1987.

Press, John. *The Chequer'd Shade: Reflections on Obscurity in Poetry.* New York: Oxford University Press, 1958.

Qualey, Elizabeth Cummings. *When I Was a Little Girl.* Center Ossippee, N.H.: Carrol County Independent, 1981.

Reck, Michael. Review of *Fairy Tales. Commonweal* 1 (February 1966): 562.

Rotella, Guy. *E. E. Cummings: A Reference Guide.* Boston: G. K. Hall, 1979.

———. "E. E. Cummings: A Reference Guide Updated." *Resources for American Literary Study* 12, no. 2 (Autumn 1982 [1985]): 143–88.

———. "E. E. Cummings: A Reference Guide (Again) Updated." *SPRING: The Journal of the E. E. Cummings Society* 1, no. 1 (October 1992): 127–43; no. 2 (October 1993): 107–23.

"The Scourge of the Unpeople." Review of *Selected Letters. Times Literary Supplement* (November 17, 1972): 1403.

Shapiro, Karl. Review of *Selected Letters. Bookworld* 3 (July 6, 1969).

Tanner, James E. Jr. "The Grammar of Poetry." Ph.D. diss., University of North Carolina, 1973.

Triem, Eve. *E. E. Cummings.* Pamphlet. Minneapolis: University of Minnesota, 1969.

Tucker, Robert. "Cummings the Chivalrous." In *The Twenties*, edited by R. E. Langford and W. E. Taylor. Deland, Fla.: Everett Edwards, 1966.

Wagner-Martin, Linda. "Cummings' *Him*—and Me." *SPRING: The Journal of the E. E. Cummings Society.* 1, no. 1 (October 1992): 28–36.

———. "E. E. Cummings: A Review of the Research and Criticism." *Resources for American Literary Study* 11, no. 2 (Autumn 1981): 184–214.

Wain, John. "An Idiom of Desperation." In *Hopkins: A Collection of Critical Essays*, edited by Geoffrey Hartman, 57–70. Englewood Cliffs, N.J.: Prentice-Hall, 1966.

Watson, Hildegarde Lasell. *The Edge of the Woods.* Lunenburg, Vt.: Stinehour Press, 1979.

Wegner, Robert E. *The Poetry and Prose of E. E. Cummings.* New York: Harcourt, Brace, and World, 1965.

Whitehead, Alfred North. *Science and the Modern World.* New York: Macmillan, 1939.

index